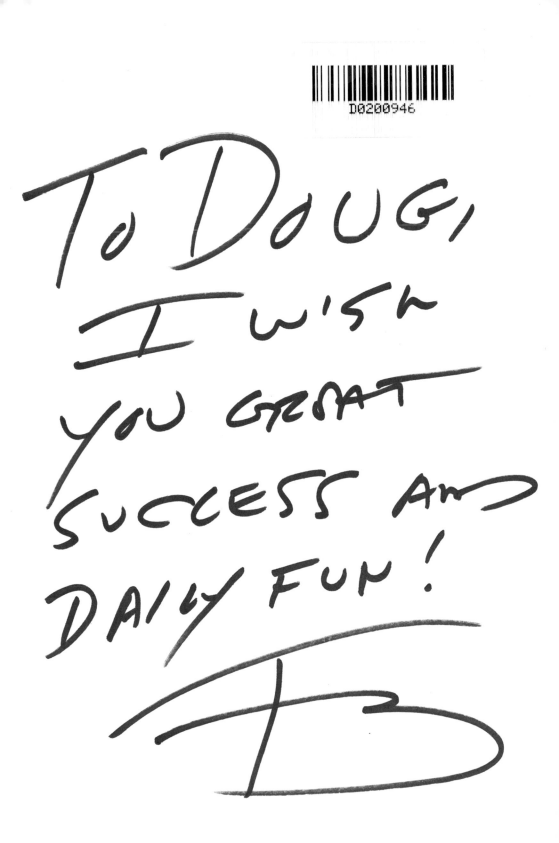

D0200946

To Doug,

I wish you great success and daily fun!

Everything is Marketing:

THE ULTIMATE STRATEGY FOR DENTAL PRACTICE GROWTH

Fifth Edition

Fred Joyal

FOUNDER OF 1-800-DENTIST®

with a foreword by Linda Miles

Copyright © 2014 Futuredontics, Inc.

ISBN: 9780615940854

Printed in the United States of America

Editor: Brian Becker
Jacket Design: Shane Beers
Jacket Photography: Arthur Gu
Graphics: Jill Teeples
Photos: Fred Joyal
Text Design: Soundview Design Studio

All literary material appearing in this publication is the property of Futuredontics, Inc. It is protected by U.S. copyright laws and is not to be reproduced, disseminated, published or transferred in any form or by any means, without prior written permission from Futuredontics, Inc. Requests to the copyright holder for permission should be addressed to Futuredontics, Inc., 6060 Center Drive, 7th Floor, Los Angeles, California 90045. Copyright infringement is a violation of federal law subject to criminal and civil penalties. All Rights Reserved.

Limit of Liability/Disclaimer of Warranty: While the publisher and author have used their best efforts in preparing this book, they make no representations or warranties with respect to the accuracy or completeness of the contents of this book and specifically disclaim any implied warranties of merchantability or fitness for a particular purpose. No warranty may be created or extended by sales representatives or written sales materials. The advice and strategies contained herein may not be suitable for your situation. You should consult with a professional where appropriate. Neither the publisher nor author shall be liable for any loss of profit or any other commercial damages, including but not limited to special, incidental, consequential or other damages.

ATTENTION CONSULTANTS, CORPORATIONS, UNIVERSITIES, COLLEGES AND PROFESSIONAL ORGANIZATIONS:
Quantity discounts are available on bulk purchases of this book for educational or training purposes. It is also available as an audio book. For information please contact Futuredontics, Inc. at the address below.

Fifth Hardcover Edition
Published by Futuredontics, Inc.
6060 Center Drive, 7th Floor
Los Angeles, CA 90045
(866) 903-9403
www.futuredontics.com

To Mira.
Anyone who knows her knows why.

CONTENTS

SECTION TWO: Refining Your Marketing

SECTION THREE: Refining Your Advertising

FOREWORD

Fred Joyal, the Ambassador of Dental Marketing, has "hit it over the fence" with this book. Little did Fred know back when the book was just a figment of his imagination (in his mind and heart), that soon after he started writing it, our country would enter into the biggest recession since 1929. If you read and follow a few principles in this book, the investment will bring tens of thousands of dollars in increased monthly revenues, not to mention the satisfaction of building stronger relationships with patients and coworkers in the process. After all, creating a happier work environment is what this book is about. And as Fred clearly points out: Patients who get what they expected *return*, patients who get less than they expected *leave*, and patients who get more than they expected *refer*. Fred's company, 1-800-DENTIST®, has taught this concept to more people in our profession than anyone else in dentistry.

When I first heard Fred lecture at the AADOM (American Association of Dental Office Managers) Conference in Tampa, Florida, I could hardly sit still as a participant. (That is something very hard for all speakers to do...listen to another speaker.) I wanted to high-five him for what he was saying. It was amazing how alike we thought on so many marketing principles. Fred is so right! Marketing is in everything, from the signage out front, to the image of the reception area, to the business and clinical team, to the smells, sounds and technology. It is all part of the marketing package.

We also agree that the telephone is the most important instrument in the practice and that the person answering it can make or break the business by their behavior—the way they answer the phone, greet patients and their tone of empathy and kindness (or the lack thereof). It's also amazing to both Fred and most management consultants how many practices view emergencies as a fate worse than death. These practices only want "A" patients. When I sat at the front desk of my last dental employer, it was my job to connect each caller to the dentistry they deserved. It wasn't my job to pre-judge the patients and only allow in those whom I felt were worthy of my doctor's wonderful care. My goal was to treat emergencies as well as established patients. I soon discovered these emergency patients became the practice's biggest referral sources.

This book will also dispel the myth that marketing is expensive. It will convince each reader that marketing and practice management are closely related, and it will prove to one and all that once each practice has created a caring and professionally fun work environment, dentists and team members will not only produce more, but they will also look forward to each work day.

I recommend that this book become an in-office training guide on marketing and management. Each team member and doctor should have their own copy of the book to highlight, dog-ear and study time and again to not only get on the right track, but to stay on track. Read a chapter every week and make a list of your two best ideas from that chapter. Over a weekly team lunch, discuss how you can use that chapter to make your practice better for patients, the doctors and everyone on the team. Books like this one are meant to be used, not read once and placed on a bookshelf to grow dusty.

To Fred Joyal, and all the folks at 1-800-DENTIST, thanks for giving our profession the exposure to the outside world with your advertising of quality dentistry and wonderful training for the dental team. And thanks, Fred, for this shot in the arm from your many years of perfecting what does and does not work well in dentistry. Practices for the next 20 years will be recession-proof if they start now and follow your sage advice in the months and years to come.

Linda Miles

Linda Miles, CSP, CMC, is the founder of LLM&A and the Speaking Consulting Network. She is an internationally renowned consultant, speaker and author on the topics of staff development and dental practice management.

INTRODUCTION

A lot has changed since I first wrote this book in 2008. America was deep in the throes of the recession and dentistry was undergoing a painful metamorphosis as a business model. Where the goal had once been to become a completely insurance-free practice, now dentists by the hundreds were simply walking away from their practices, unable to make the next bank loan payment.

Also, credit was tighter than the door on the space shuttle. Facebook was for college kids. Mobile phones were for phone calls, and people actually checked their voicemail. Yelp was still on the drawing board. And parts of the country had 50 percent of mortgages under water, and others had unemployment as high as the Great Depression. And to top it all off, there were no iPads.

Today, it's a new world. Our economy is recovering in fits and starts, with new areas of the country thriving and others filing for bankruptcy. Health care is embroiled in a major and indecipherable flux. And dental insurance companies are turning on their creators in an almost mythical betrayal.

And it's a digital-dominated world. Sixty percent of Internet searches now begin on mobile phones. Virtually everyone has an email address, and the fastest-growing group of Facebook users is over 60. More than half of consumers seek online reviews before making a purchase. And the amount of time we spend online has *doubled* in the past three years.[1] Never in history has human behavior changed so fast.

And more people than ever are neglecting their teeth. The disposable income for the middle and lower classes seems to have been gobbled up by oil companies, tuition and sales tax. People rely either on insurance or the emergency room for their dentistry in escalating numbers every year.

And finding the cheapest thing is as easy as asking your phone. And yet, many people don't want the cheapest everything. They still want quality. They want service. They want to be genuinely cared for and treated well. Businesses like Zappos and Apple thrive by having the best service and the best products, not the lowest prices.

This book has evolved with each stage of these shifting sands. This will be the fourth revision. Two-thirds of the book is similar to the first edition, but the last third—how you advertise, promote your practice and communicate with your patients—has changed dramatically, as have the number of services that my company now offers.

As ever, I am optimistic. Interest rates have stayed lower than anyone ever predicted. The U.S. population is growing faster than the respective population of dentists. Technology is making it possible for practices to deliver care faster, better and more affordably. And the baby boomers are inheriting the largest transfer of wealth in the history of mankind.

Dentists who have evolved with the times are finding that theirs is still one of the most rewarding professions. And thousands of dentists and team members have found this book to be the catalyst for positive and permanent change. That is very gratifying to me, because my intention was not just for folks to read the book, but to apply it. And the feedback I get helps me improve it with every revision.

This book is dedicated to you: the smart, hard-working teams who show up every day to help people be more healthy. I wish you continued success, a greater sense of purpose, and fun and satisfaction in your day-to-day practice of this great and noble profession.

SECTION ONE:

REFINING
YOUR
MINDSET

CHAPTER 1

WHY LISTEN
TO ME?

Why the heck should you listen to me? I'm not a dentist. I don't own a dental practice, nor have I ever run one.

The answer is simply this: Your skill set is dentistry. You were offered maybe one business course in all your years of dental school, and you skipped it because you were focused (quite reasonably) on passing your clinicals. Even if you did attend, they barely talked about marketing or advertising. And today you need 30-40 hours of CE every year just to keep up with changes in cosmetics, implants, bonding agents, radiography and the constant wave of new technologies.

My skill set is not dentistry. It's advertising and marketing, specifically focused on getting people to go to the dentist. That's what I spend all my time doing, what I study and what I'm constantly refining. It's my career. At the risk of sounding immodest, I don't believe there is anyone in dentistry with my level of experience in marketing. (It's a pretty narrow field of players to stay ahead of.)

To begin with, I've worked in advertising since 1980, starting at a major advertising agency, writing television and radio commercials as well as print ads, and generally learning how advertising works: how it is created, how it is placed, as well as how it is used by businesses. I saw what succeeded, what failed and what simply never moved the needle.

Then I got into the dental field. In 1986, my partner Gary Saint Denis and I started Futuredontics, Inc., the parent company of 1-800-DENTIST, in Los Angeles, which expanded over the years to become the largest dental referral service in the country. To date, we have spent more than half a billion dollars promoting the brand. I have personally written over 200 television and radio ads to prompt consumers to call our phone number and visit our website. Along the way, we have tried every medium and approach: cable and network television, radio, print, billboards, bus cards, newspapers, magazines, airplane banners, direct mail, and on the Internet we have multiple websites and bid on more than 1,000,000 keywords in any given month. We even do ads on mobile phones. We track in minute detail which messages work with consumers and which ones don't.

As a result, we get thousands of people calling us every single day across the country, and tens of thousands coming to our websites. Over the years, we have referred literally millions of people to dentists who are members of our service. But even more importantly, we operate a live call center in Los Angeles, 24/7, 365 days a year. I learn more about the dental consumer in one day listening in on phone calls than I could get out of a dozen books on consumer behavior.

We also survey all of the people who have called us or found a dentist through us online and ask them about their experience at the dentist's office. You would be amazed at the time some people will spend crafting a response. Some of them are two pages long. And we have accumulated thousands of them over the years.

Because of all these interactions, we have a clear sense of what people want from you. They tell us their needs, their wants and their fears—and we listen. We have learned the reasons people avoid the dentist, what they are looking for in a dentist, what finally gets them to see a dentist and what turns them off (or on) about dental practices.

Something else also happens. Because we directly connect referrals to the dental office, we communicate with each of our members' appointment coordinators almost every day, and those interactions are equally instructive.

Finally, it's important to know that because of this business, I've also been involved with some of the most successful dental practices in the country—from solo practitioners who produce $2 million annually in middle class neighborhoods, to practices thriving in remote parts of the country, to dentists in highly competitive areas who enjoy extraordinary success while their peers struggle. I've also seen practices that do things wrong and never get out of the painful cycle of fluctuating income and profit. I've taken all of these experiences and distilled them down into some powerful techniques for bringing your office to a whole different level.

Interested? Then read on.

CHAPTER 2

THE DIFFERENCE
BETWEEN MARKETING
AND ADVERTISING

Most people, including many businesspeople, think marketing and advertising are the same thing. They're not. I'll explain the difference, but first let me introduce this very important fact to you: If your marketing doesn't work, your advertising doesn't stand a chance.

Let's start with some basic definitions. Advertising is using a specific medium—the newspaper, radio, TV or Internet— to communicate who you are and what your practice does. Marketing is *everything* you do to communicate who you are and what you do. This includes obvious things like on-hold messages and much less obvious things like the color of your reception area. It's an important distinction.

Here is an abbreviated list of aspects of your practice that constitute your practice marketing:

- The smell of your office
- How you answer the phone
- Your patient intake forms
- Your technology
- How you collect money

Some of these items may not make sense yet. They will, and I'll go into each one eventually. But implicit in this list is the big secret: Everything is marketing. Okay, it's not a big secret since it happens to be the title of the book, but my main point is that every physical aspect and everything that happens in your practice has some element of marketing to it. And many things that you are not focused on are having a subtle effect, and sometimes a huge effect, on your patients—both their perception of you and their receptivity to treatment.

This is a book about marketing much more so than about advertising. That's because the advertising part is easy. "Easy?! Not for me it isn't," you say. But, in my experience with hundreds of dental practices all over the country, it is not the advertising of the practice that is failing, it is the marketing. Spending on advertising while neglecting your marketing is like putting a bridge between two unstable teeth. It may work for a while, but it's not really doing what it's supposed to, and in the end the effort is likely to fail.

"If your marketing doesn't work, your advertising doesn't stand a chance."

To illustrate where dentistry is, let me tell you the story of a certain unique individual. In early 1950, a young father was sitting on a bench at a county fair with his daughter, thinking to himself, "This place is dirty; the rides don't seem safe; and the people working here seem like criminals. There has to be something better for my family."

That man happened to be Walt Disney. He decided to make the cleanest, safest amusement park possible, with happy employees, good food and great service. And in the process, he changed everyone's perception of family entertainment. I submit to you that for at least half the population, the perception of dentistry is in need of the same radical change. Too many people are afraid of a dental visit. More precisely, they associate dentistry with pain, medieval equipment and an uncaring professional who provides a necessary evil—one that is to be avoided until the last possible moment.

We all know that's not accurate. And I know you're saying, "My patients don't think that." True. The people I'm talking about generally aren't anybody's patients. But you can't pretend that there isn't a large segment of the population that would rather be audited by the IRS than see a dentist. It's ignorance. And the only way to cure ignorance is with knowledge.

Consider Walt Disney's approach. He thought about every sight, sound, smell and taste, and asked how he could transform them into something positive and memorable. That's marketing. More importantly, it's an example of what dentistry can become, and it's what this book is all about.

Just like Disneyland®, where you don't even notice most of the marketing magic that is built into the place, there are essential aspects of your practice, both good and bad, that are aggregating to a very powerful set of impressions. Before we're done, I hope to have you rethinking your entire practice. Some things you may already be doing right (you're not broke, right? Something's working!). But small changes can have profound, long-lasting results. And the more you get all these marketing aspects aligned with the message you want to send, the more your practice will spiral upwards, both in terms of production and enjoyment.

Let's just take one marketing aspect from the previous list that probably jumped out at you. How can the way you *collect money* be marketing? Simple. It communicates how you value yourself and your work. This is huge. In marketing, perceived value is almost more important than real value. A Lexus® is probably every bit the car, both in technology and amenities, as the equivalent size Mercedes-Benz®. But try getting a Benz for the same price. If you bill patients and let them pay when they feel like it, if you discount your fees, if you spend hours each week just trying to collect your money, then you are communicating something very specific to the public and to your patients—and it's probably not the message you want transmitted.

Think about other industries where this is done. Hotels have been insisting on a credit card to make a reservation for years, and now the best ones debit your card when you check in for the amount you *might* spend on incidentals. They want to make sure you can pay for those expensive cashews ahead of time. High-end restaurants are starting to ask for a credit card number with your reservation, and they will charge you if you don't show up. Many of them also get a phone number, and if you don't show up for your reservation, then you go on a "Don't Reserve" list. Why? Because their tables are valuable, and seating is, as we call it in marketing, a *wasting commodity*. In other words, if they don't use it that night, they never get that seating back. Kind of like your office. Except you'll let patients cancel at the last minute and put a hole in your appointment schedule without charging them. In this behavior, you've effectively taught them that your time is less valuable than theirs. Remember, everything you do, intentional or unintentional, communicates something to the patient.

Here's the most painful comparison. Call a plumber to your house and try not paying him when he's done—ask to be billed. How do you think that will go? "But wait," you say, "My treatments are a lot more expensive than a plumber's, so my patients can't pay right away." Really? My last plumbing bill was $8,000 to put a new main water line to the house from the street. Half was paid up front, and half the second they finished. So here is the real message you're communicating: Plumbing is more valuable than my dentistry. Thus you have receivables, and you probably end up writing off 10 percent of them.

Conversely, I was recently in the dental practice of my friend, Dr. Greg Sawyer, who focuses mostly on doing implants, and he collects 100 percent of the fee *before* he starts the case. Not half. *All of it.* If the patients don't have the money, he waits until they do to start treatment. If they have the funds but don't want to pay upfront, this tells him that they don't understand everything about the procedure, or they don't value his time. He explains that he can only start cases when patients are fully committed to completing the treatment, and that he has considerable upfront expenses in the process. Then he treats the people who are ready to pay. And his practice is booming.

Of course, how you collect money is just one tiny element of your overall practice marketing, but I hope you can see the real effect this one little aspect has. And the reason I am driving this point home so strongly is because I constantly hear dentists saying that they need more patients, or better advertising, when the truth is that most of the advertising they do is wasted because their marketing and internal processes are severely impacting the results of that promotion. I'll go much more into how a comprehensive approach to marketing fixes this. But remember: 90 percent of dental advertising fails not because of the ad, but because of what happens *after* the ad runs.

Most dentists hope that their advertising brings in new patients who just fly into the chair with their mouths and their wallets wide open. There is no ad that good, no direct mail piece that effective, no TV commercial that persuasive, no Yellow Pages™ ad that can have that powerful an effect. All advertising can do is bring somebody to your phone or your door, and the rest of it is really up to you. And "the rest" is the really important part.

Think of this process like a funnel. The wider it is at the bottom, the more patients can get through. Advertising tells a bunch of people what you do. A small percentage respond. Some appoint. Some of them show up. And most of those, hopefully, accept treatment. The more you decrease the flow—the more you narrow the funnel at each level with ineffective marketing—the fewer people who will actually make it into your practice and accept treatment. (See Figure 1.)

Figure 1

ADVERTISING RESULTS

PEOPLE WHO SEE YOUR ADVERTISING

PEOPLE WHO RESPOND

PEOPLE WHO MAKE AN APPT.

PEOPLE WHO SHOW UP

PEOPLE WHO ACCEPT TREATMENT

Let me tell you a story that one of our members, Dr. Tim Driscoll in Chicago, told me. It was Friday, late in the day. When the staff was leaving the office around 5 o'clock, they said, "Dr. Driscoll, there's a woman in the parking lot who keeps getting in and out of her car."

So he went out to look. Sure enough, he saw a very agitated woman getting out of her car and, after a moment, getting right back in again. He walked over to her and said, "Hi, I'm Dr. Driscoll. Can I help you in any way?"

She answered, "You know, I desperately need to see a dentist and I'm absolutely terrified. But I'm in so much pain I don't know what to do." Tim told her, "I've had a lot of patients just like you who have been really afraid. Come on in. I can help you."

When she finally came into his office and sat down in the operatory, he found out she hadn't seen a dentist in 30 years and *she hadn't left her house in eight!* Her dental neglect had made her a complete shut-in. Her mouth was a masterpiece of decay, horror and pain. Dr. Driscoll got one of his assistants to stay late with him, and he worked until 10 o'clock that night on the patient. He had to extract some of her teeth, and had to remove a lot of decay in others. He did as much restorative work as possible that night. He has a CEREC® unit in his office, which allowed him to restore some teeth, and he used a laser on much of the soft tissue and infection problems.

By the end of the night she was hardly finished, but he sent her home out of pain and with a noticeably more normal-looking smile. He made an appointment for her to return that Monday so that he could continue.

That next Monday morning, she showed up in the office looking completely different. Her hair was colored and coiffed. She had new, stylish clothes. She was wearing makeup. And she was just beaming. When he saw her, Dr. Driscoll immediately noticed the radical change. "Wow, you look great!" he said. "What happened?"

She answered, "You know, I hadn't been out of the house in over eight years. This Saturday my daughter and I went out. We went to the hair salon, we went to the nail salon, we went to the makeup counter at Nordstrom®, and we bought three new outfits for me. It's just been incredible. I just feel so much better."

Then she said, "I have a thank you card for you because you saved my life. I was at a point where I was either going to finally see a dentist or commit suicide, and I honestly didn't know which one I was going to choose. I was so scared, but I was in so much pain, and I was trapped in my house. So thank you for that, because you've made it possible for me to live."

Needless to say, Dr. Driscoll never forgot this remarkable and gratifying moment.

Along with the powerful emotional impact, there are several marketing aspects to this story—that is, things that happened after the patient saw an ad and found Dr. Driscoll's address. First, his staff noticed a patient outside the practice—team awareness and caring are absolutely elements of marketing. Then he talked to her empathetically by saying, "I've helped people just like you." The words you use are key factors in your practice marketing. He very effectively used words that allayed her fears and told her she wasn't alone. Then he stayed the entire evening to get her out of pain—a professional choice, but it reflects a marketing decision that includes being available, dealing with emergencies with compassion and doing something totally unexpected for a patient. His technology—a laser and a CEREC unit—are dental tools, but they are marketing tools as well. And it all adds up to a level of marketing effectiveness that will get him literally hundreds of new patients in the end. I have no doubt about that. By the end of this book, you shouldn't have any either.

I think the most important message in Dr. Driscoll's story is this: This is your profession. This is what you can do in your practice. You can reach into someone's life at this low, low point and transform her in a matter of days. What an exciting job to have. What an exciting place to show up to every day. Be excited about it. Tell people what you do. Tell people the difference you can make in their lives. That's all marketing is, effectively telling people what you can do for them. The key word is *effectively*.

And if you don't believe that this is what your profession is all about, then that is precisely where you need to start. You need to fix your own mindset. If you don't believe that for a patient in need of major restorative care, $20,000 is better spent in their mouth than on anything else they can think of, then that's your first problem, because that's the fact. You need to realize it, believe it, make it part of your being, be proud of it and surround yourself with a team that believes exactly the same thing.

So let's address this mindset, because it's the only way to get the marketing started off right. And the first stage of this is to actually understand what type of business you are in.

CHAPTER 3

THE UNIQUE
BUSINESS OF
DENTISTRY

A dental practice is a weird business. The manager/owner has to be working with his hands in order to be making money. In most other businesses, like mine, managers *manage*. That's what we do all day, and if I stop managing for a day or two, my business, and I, keep making money. Not true for dentists. When your hands stop, the revenue stops. And to top it off, where do you get the training to run your business on the financial side, or to do effective advertising, or to hire, train and manage employees? Not in dental school, that's for sure. Also, consider the fact that the public sees you one way, as a maintenance service provider, but you see yourself as an engineer and entrepreneur. Contradictory? To say the least. Now let's go even deeper into the basic nature of your business.

What do you consider the true economic nature of a dental practice? In other words, essentially what type of business are

you in? Is it a medical facility? Is it some sort of insurance provider? Is it a repair shop for teeth? The answer is very different from what you might guess based on the way most dental
practices behave.

The answer to this question came to me when I was on vacation,
taking a trip down the Amazon River. We were traveling into
some of the more remote regions, where very primitive tribes
still live their entire lives alongside the river, almost completely
detached from the rest of civilization. As we putted along in
our riverboat, we encountered another boat that was going from
village to village with a dentist and his assistant on board, along
with various other medical professional volunteers.

The villagers were eagerly awaiting this dentist's arrival. And
what did they want? Did they want a prophy? A little deep
scaling? PFMs on those cracked and decayed teeth? Of course
not. They wanted extractions, because pulling the tooth would
solve the immediate problem. It's hardly the standard of care
we aspire to in the United States. But the fact of the matter
is, in three quarters of the world that's how tooth problems
are solved. And it's pretty close to what most insurance plans
believe if you look at their schedule of benefits. That's when it
dawned on me: *Everything beyond extraction is elective.*

I'm sure you're saying to yourself, "Yep. Extraction, that's not
our standard of care." But keep in mind that 25 percent of the
US population over 65 is edentulous.[2] 25 percent! They're not
all just falling out. Somebody's pulling lots of teeth right here
in the good old USA.

So if everything beyond extraction is elective, then what does that mean? It means you are in a service profession with a significant retail element, because people have options. If all the things you do beyond pulling the tooth are, to some degree, a higher standard of care, you are in a *retail service profession.* Now many dentists will cringe at this notion. They'll say, "I'm a professional. I'm not running a store. People come to me for what they need and I give them the highest standard of care." That would be true if people actually came to you for what they need. But most of the time they come to you for as little as possible, which you and I know is *not* what they need. Nor is it what they should want. They have a range of options, from basic to ideal care—and those choices are constantly increasing with new techniques and technologies. And those choices are mostly elective. In fact, statistics show that less than half of dentists' revenue is paid by insurance companies each year. The rest, the patients pay themselves.[3]

Dentists are definitely not like most other health care businesses. You're in a unique category that's very different from, say, a physician. Let me illustrate my point: If you break your arm anywhere in North America, they will put your arm in a cast. No one is going to cut your arm off. No one is going to whip out a laser and heal the bone. But if you walk into a dental practice with a sore tooth, any one of a half a dozen procedures could be performed, from a simple extraction to placing an implant. Your business model is much more like that of a dermatologist or a plastic surgeon, where there are a variety of treatment options, most of them elective.

I hope you will appreciate that what I'm saying is true, and that you will also come to realize that a retail business model is not a bad thing, but a wonderful opportunity.

In fact, the options for different levels of care in dentistry are actually a professional advantage. You can either take good care of people, or take really good care of them. And let's face it, you really don't want to be a health care provider if it means you're just an insurance provider. You don't want people coming to you expecting everything to be paid for by insurance, which is what 95 percent of MDs currently experience. It's an important distinction. It's also one of the reasons why being a dentist is actually better, in my mind, than being an MD. Your life is not controlled by insurance. Also, you're not getting paged 24 hours a day. Finally, and not insignificantly, as of 2005 the average income of an MD is lower than the average income of a dentist.[4] This trend will continue, especially with universal health care on the horizon.

So what does being in a retail service profession mean to your practice? It means that to maximize your success, everyone in your practice has to be selling dentistry. I know, I used a bad word here. I said "selling." Dentists hate the idea of selling. I hear it all the time. "I don't want to have to sell. I didn't get into this profession to sell." It's really more that you don't like the negative connotation of a salesperson. You didn't go to dental school to become some kind of carnival barker. I understand that. But I also said, "to maximize your success." I know many dentists who bumble along doing 80 percent of things wrong from a business standpoint who still make a living. But it's not a great living—not what it could be—and their practice will be worth a lot less when they eventually try to sell it.

So I implore you, please don't buy into the negative connotation of selling. Selling is merely *communication with a purpose*. And the simple fact is that as human beings we're selling all the time. We're selling when we're convincing our spouse that she really wants to go to Scotland and not Gettysburg for vacation (because we want to try golfing where it was invented). A baby's crying is definitely communication with a purpose. And is there anyone who sells harder than a teenage boy trying to get the car keys? He's going to wash the car, put gas in it, run an errand for you. Sell, sell, sell. And is it not a sell job to convince that same teenager that he needs to go to college instead of taking that construction job? He wants to jump into the workforce, but you know darn well that he needs a college degree if he's going to realize his dreams. So you sell. And is that a bad thing? Not at all. Selling bad things is bad. Selling phony oil and gas leases to little old ladies is bad. Selling illegal drugs is bad. Selling something good is…well, good. And I think we can all agree that dentistry is a good thing.

Remember, selling is merely communication with a purpose. In your case, that purpose is convincing a person to do what you know they should to take proper care of their teeth. Is proper dental care not a wise long-term investment? As I said in the last chapter, if you don't believe that money spent in their mouth is a better investment than almost anything else they can spend it on, *that's* your problem. Because you don't believe in what you're selling. And that makes it very, very difficult.

I've had sales jobs all my life, in one form or another. In my early years, one of my jobs was selling frozen meat door to door. Part of the whole package included selling the customer a big freezer, and I helped them finance the whole thing—the freezer and a three-month supply of frozen meat and vegetables. The problem was, in order for the food to last, they had to eat very controlled portions. And it was the highest quality beef available. Prime. The customers loved it, and so they ate it fast, and in big portions. And then they had to order more while still making payments on the first shipment. Do you see where this was going? I was selling something that was too expensive for the people I was selling to, and I was trained to wrap the whole deal in a deceptive package so that they would buy. As soon as I figured that out, I couldn't sell anymore. I had started out believing it was great food at a reasonable price, but once I didn't believe in it anymore, I was dead. So I quit.

In a dental practice, you don't have that problem. You have something truly great to sell. But if you don't want to call it selling, call it something else. Call it *facilitating treatment acceptance*. It's a nice way of saying the same thing (we love euphemisms in advertising!). And when you think about it, that's what you're really doing. You're helping a patient who has no understanding of the value of dentistry to accept the treatment that you know is the best standard of care for them. Perhaps you just haven't made this connection in your mind yet. You haven't thought about the fact that your patients' lives are going to be significantly better with the comprehensive care that you recommend. And you worry that they won't really appreciate the value.

"Don't look at it as selling; look at it as facilitating treatment acceptance."

This lack of appreciation of the value of dentistry is why I'm going to suggest to you that facilitating treatment acceptance is not only something you need to do to succeed financially; I'm suggesting that it is actually your professional responsibility. Most people have not been properly educated by anyone as to the value of dental care. Not in school, not at home, not at work. You have the chance to help them understand how to achieve optimum oral health and make the decision to do so. After all, if you don't do it, who will? Do you think perhaps they'll eventually talk themselves into it? Unfortunately, that's just not the case.

In reality, patients usually need to be dragged kicking and screaming from their desire to get as little dentistry as possible (kind of like the Amazon tribesmen) to accepting some level of care beyond that. In sales and marketing we call this process—taking a client (patient) from a basic service or product to a better one—an *upsell*. "Oh, great," you say, "I don't even want to be selling, and now I'm *upselling*?!" Yes. You are the one with the extensive clinical training and the knowledge base that dictates what is best to preserve their dentition. So it is you who must move them from where they are in their minds (wanting the least possible treatment at the cheapest possible price) to accepting your standard of care or your ideal treatment plan. And it may take years.

At least half the time the patient will need to figure out how to pay for this level of care, because either they don't have insurance or insurance doesn't cover what is optimal. That is also very different from almost every medical practice except dermatology and plastic surgery. And the way those two specialties operate offers some good insights into what dentistry can become, and the way to get there. If you have a chance to observe one of these professions, look at all of the options they offer. Look at how they collect money. Look at how they explain the value of the treatment. And you have something to offer that they don't: Your treatment is going to keep people eating, smiling and kissing freely into old age.

Dentistry involves selling. Plain, simple and unavoidable. And the better you and your team are at facilitating the acceptance of treatment, the more profitable your practice will be, and the happier and healthier your patients will be. There's nothing wrong or evil or deceptive about that. With the realization that you are in a retail service profession, you can emulate what many successful retail services do. That involves comprehensive, effective marketing. But it always starts with the right mindset.

So why would you do this? Why would you summon these skills? Why would you adopt this mindset? Why can't you just go along with what you're doing? The fact of the matter is—you can. If you're happy with your income, if you're happy with your practice size and if you keep up with technology enough, you'll probably be fine. You won't change your patients' opinion of the importance of dentistry and you won't experience the potential for tremendous success in your practice. But why not indulge me for a bit? Wouldn't you rather have a more enjoyable day? And can you really go back to ignorance and denial? It won't be easy. I may have taken you a bit too far behind the curtain, and I'm afraid there's no going back.

A CASE STUDY

Let me tell you about two 1-800-DENTIST members. I'll protect their anonymity and protect myself from any HIPAA violations by calling them Dr. Minnie and Dr. Max. They live in very similar demographic areas, essentially middle class neighborhoods. They're both in a little under 1,800 square feet of office space. Also, they both are solo practitioners. The first practice, Dr. Minnie, has six operatories and eight staff members. She works an average of 18 days a month, takes four weeks off a year, and gets 60 hours of continuing education every year. She has a pretty good life and a pretty good practice. Dr. Minnie's gross and net are a little bit higher than what the ADA says the average full-time dentist does. She's doing $600,000 annually. Her overhead is about 70 percent, which is also typical at that level of production, so she's taking home $180,000 per year.

Dr. Max has seven staff members, one less than Dr. Minnie. He works only 15 days a month, not 18, and takes six weeks off a year. He gets twice as much CE, about 120 hours. And he produces $2.5 million annually. But his overhead, and this is one of the wonderful things about dentistry, is 50 percent. He also grows at about 10 percent per year. So he takes home $1.25 million per year, more than twice Dr. Minnie's gross production. And he does it in three days less a month and two weeks less a year. (See Figure 2.)

Figure 2

PRACTICE POTENTIAL

Dr. Minnie	Dr. Max
6 operatories	6 operatories
8 staff members	7 staff members
18 days a month	15 days a month
4 weeks off a year	6 weeks off a year
60 hours of CE	120 hours of CE
$600,000 annually	$2.5 million annually
70% overhead	50% overhead
$180,000 profit	$1.25 million profit

So what's going on? What is Dr. Max doing that Dr. Minnie isn't? What's different about their practices? Some of you may say that Dr. Max must be over-diagnosing. But if that were true, then explain how he could over-diagnose all of his patients year after year and still have them not only accept treatment, but also recommend their friends and family to the practice? Because that is what's happening in his office. It comes down to this: In Dr. Max's practice, *every single person believes and communicates that dentistry can change people's lives.*

Now, every word in that statement is important. Every single person—not just the dentist, not just the front desk, not just the hygienist, not 90 percent of the staff, but everyone—believes and communicates that dentistry can change people's lives. They not only *believe* it, they *communicate* it. And the message is not that dentistry can keep patients' mouths healthy, not that it can make their teeth white or get them out of their immediate discomfort. The message is that it can *change their lives*. That's the core belief that you and your team have to start with. This is the exact mindset that I see time and again in the most successful practices across the country. What is also significant is that these practices have a great time. They enjoy their day. And the dentists can afford not only the best and latest technology but also tons of CE. So they get faster and more skilled all the time. They also have the income and the lifestyle that they want—and far exceed that of most dentists and physicians.

There is another aspect of your business that is valuable to note here. There is a marketing distinction that describes in part how you are perceived by the consuming public. You are either a *parity* service, or you are *singular*. In other words, there are competitors that essentially offer exactly what you do, or there are none (because of a patent or something else that makes the service unique). Toilet paper is a parity product. Airlines are a parity service. Obviously, within those categories each brand has some differences, but they are minor relative to the fundamental product or service. Viagra®, when it first came out, was singular. It had no competitor, and it rapidly became one of the largest selling pharma-

> "Everyone in the practice should believe and communicate that dentistry can change people's lives."

ceuticals in the world. Now it has competitors, and has started to become a parity product.

Why am I babbling on about this? Simply because, in the public's mind, dentistry is a parity service. They can get the same services at any one of a hundred dental offices around them. *Or so they believe.* Now, there are only two ways to compete in a parity service business: price or features. And either one of these has to be communicated over and over again to the consumer. That's what advertising is all about, and why it's everywhere. Most products and services are parity in nature, and realizing this will help you to understand that you have to effectively communicate the differences between your practice and the other offices around you. And you'd better *have* differences.

The advantage you have is that when you do something unique, or you give a patient a memorable experience in your practice, then you are no longer providing a parity service in their mind. The opportunity is there to completely change their perception. And of course, marketing is the key.

TWO IMPORTANT DIFFERENCES

Despite being a parity service and a retail profession, dentistry has two unique and highly advantageous business characteristics. One relates to profitability and the other concerns the target audience—that is, the potential customers.

Compared to other businesses, dentistry has a unique overhead and profitability structure. I've found that many dentists don't fully appreciate this. They don't really understand the economics of their practice because they just let their accountant figure that out. But there is a term in economics called a *contribution margin ratio*. Let me explain.

Most businesses operate with 10 or 15 percent profit margin. No matter how big they get, they're still squeezing out that amount of profit. Supermarkets run at a 3 percent profit margin. Imagine how hard that is when there is such a high level of competition everywhere giving out coupons on everything. They have to sell $35 million in groceries to make a million in profit. And the margins don't get better as they make more money. That's a tough business.

Dentistry is completely different. You have a unique ratio of fixed expenses versus variable expenses. Once you cover your overhead—your rent, insurance, utilities, leases, loans and basic salaries—your profit margins get significantly better. This usually occurs at around $600,000 in production. It's also why most dentists don't appreciate this economic reality, because that's what the average dental practice is grossing. Think about it, though. The simple fact is that once your overhead is paid, you only have labs and consumables as your expenses against any production. Unless your staff is completely busy, you don't need to hire more people or pay more salary. And until you need a bigger facility, more chairs, more equipment or more space, your overhead is probably less than 30 percent on everything beyond the first $600,000, even allowing for staff bonuses.

Of course, at some point you'll need another hygienist, a front office manager or an associate. But until your schedule's full and your employees are at 100 percent utilization, your profit margin is huge. This is a tremendous advantage, and a unique one. (See Figure 3.)

Figure 3

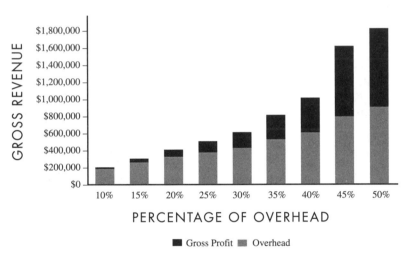

CONTRIBUTION MARGIN

Once you push beyond that $600,000, suddenly the results are dramatic. As soon as you get up around $1 million, relative to other businesses your margins are fantastic; with mostly fixed costs, your overhead percentage continues to decrease as you add more patients. And your lifestyle can change drastically. In fact, according to a recent study, dental offices had the highest net profit margin of all industries in the United States.[5]

This contribution margin factor also means that once you achieve this level of profit, you can do more advertising—perhaps twice as much—because you have the cash to do it. And that just keeps the practice spiraling upward. The point is, you can get yourself to this point and beyond. And of course, the way you get there is first with mindset, then with marketing.

The other advantage dentists have over most businesses is what we call a *target audience*, or a pool of all potential patients. To start with, while not everyone needs a new car or a plasma TV, everyone has teeth. And everyone needs a dentist because people's teeth don't maintain themselves (except for a few Inuits who only eat seal blubber, but let's focus on the rest of the world). Unlike dentistry, most businesses are limited in their potential customers to a small portion of the general public. Some, like a private jet service for example, are so specialized that less than 0.1 percent of the population is in their target audience. Not you. The world is your target oyster.

Even better from a business standpoint (though worse from a public health standpoint), 50 percent of the population doesn't see a dentist regularly, or even at all.[6] That's half the population! Plus, of the people who do see a dentist on a regular basis, half have been under-diagnosed and were seldom presented with optimal dental care.

Imagine if half the population didn't have TVs. Or cars! What an opportunity that would be for those respective industries! Well, that opportunity is yours. There is no other business category that I can think of with this size of an under-tapped, or *un*tapped market. Then consider the many factors that limit the number of service providers in the dental industry, from the significant costs of starting up a dental practice, to the motivation, financial ability and aptitude to get into and complete dental school.

This is a point I really want to drive home. There is no scarcity in dentistry—there is only abundant opportunity. Not in every neighborhood in every city, of course, but substantially more than in any other business. To illustrate, half the population over 35 has some level of gum disease.[7] Smells like bad breath and opportunity to me. Dental practices collected a total of over $80 billion in 2008.[8] I think there is the potential for twice that—and I'll elaborate more on this in the next chapter.

So let's review the business of dentistry.

- First, it's a retail service profession, with many options for customers. This is a good thing.
- Second, it's a parity service. Make yourself unique, and this spells opportunity.
- Third, you have a fantastic contribution margin, meaning significant profits after overhead is covered.
- Fourth, the target audience is enormous.

All in all, it's a pretty darn nice business to be in, I'd say. These are major aspects of your business—now let's get into the finer points.

CHAPTER 4

THE ISSUES OF COST AND COMPETITION

THE ISSUE OF SCARCITY

In my experience in business, there are two ways of looking at things: You either see your opportunities in the marketplace as *abundant* or *scarce*. This is more than just a personality trait, like seeing the glass half empty versus half full. It's an important assessment of the industry you're in. As I touched on in the previous chapter, dentistry is without a doubt an industry of abundance for two reasons: One, half the population doesn't have a dentist; and two, a lot more than half the population doesn't yet value dentistry or truly understand what dentistry has to offer. In fact, I would say that dentistry is the most under-utilized and under-marketed service in the country.

Unfortunately, many dentists operate with the belief that there is a scarcity of patients and opportunity. Trust me, there isn't.

But it's easy to fall into the scarcity trap. Many times you struggle to keep your business growing, and you can't help but sometimes feel that forces are working against you.

I see dentists worry about a practice opening up down the street, or another office doing print ads or mailers in their neighborhood. They worry about losing their patients to these other practices. But the simple fact is, unless you're doing something terribly wrong, you'll lose more patients from people moving away than you will from some other doctor "stealing" them.

As someone whose business is finding new patients, I have a unique window into the mindset of the public, and I want to let you in on a secret that's backed up by research we did in conjunction with Harvard University some years ago: People have almost as much fear about the process of *finding* a new dentist as they do about *going* to the dentist.[9]

In other words, if they don't have a dentist, they are slow to find one, and if they have one, they are not likely to change unless they really have to. Many times they'll just stop going to one dentist and wait years before finding another. So losing patients is more likely to happen because of something you do (or don't do) than some other practice attracting them. Besides them moving away, the next most likely reason they've left your practice is that you don't offer something they want, like cosmetic procedures or a laser. Or they don't know what you *do* offer. The latter is a problem of communication—not unusual in a dental practice—and the former is something you should be able to fix either with training or by adding equipment. In other words, these factors are in your control.

This isn't true for most other businesses, simply because their marketplace is not abundant. In the car business, for example, everyone already has a car. Dealers spend all their time and money trying to get people to buy a new one. Restaurants compete daily with every other eatery. Supermarkets are busy trying to grab business from their competition because everyone is already buying food somewhere. This is the reality for almost every business in America. Their customers have to come from the competition.

Dentists alone have the opportunity to go out and find new customers without taking them from other dentists. And while not everyone needs to eat out, or drive a car, everyone needs a dentist. Everybody has a mouth. (I was going to say everyone has teeth, but we know that isn't true!) And yet nowhere near everyone has a dentist. There are literally tens of millions of potential patients you don't have to lure away from anyone else's practice. They're just out there, waiting for someone to explain to them why they should take care of their teeth.

And here's level two of my premise: I would estimate that of the 50 percent of the population who sees a dentist fairly regularly, more than half of them are getting "crown-a-year dentistry" (i.e., what the insurance will pay for), rather than what they really need to maintain a healthy mouth. We're talking literally billions of dollars in production not even diagnosed, never mind presented. They call dentists "file cabinet millionaires" and in my experience, that is true for 90 percent of practices.

YOUR TRUE COMPETITORS

One of the keys to success in business is sizing up the competition. In dentistry that can be a little tricky. First you have to ask, "Who really competes against my dental practice?" Is it the discount dental clinic down the street? Is it the high-tech aesthetic practice that just opened in the shopping mall? How about that big group practice that just opened three offices, all within 20 miles of you? Who's really competing for your dollars? The reality is, it's none of the above. Your true competition is not other dentists. It's entirely different entities, like Mercedes-Benz, Louis Vuitton®, Sony®, BOTOX®, Carnival Cruises® and, of course, Las Vegas. These are your competitors and they are doing an excellent job of convincing your patients—and more importantly, your potential patients—that their money is much better spent on these luxuries than on bringing their teeth to the optimum level of health.

Most people, particularly those successfully avoiding the dentist, associate dentistry with pain, expense and inconvenience. That's not how they think of Hawaii or a high-definition television. And if most of what you do is elective (everything beyond extraction is elective, remember?), then 9 times out of 10 they will elect to have fun and buy toys. As a rule of thumb, people would rather buy what they want than what they need. But isn't a patient better off getting an Infiniti® instead of a Benz, and investing the extra $20,000 in their mouth? Isn't the long-term value of optimal dentistry much higher than the negligible long-term value of a Las Vegas vacation? Most people never even consider that. And the reason is simple. Mercedes and Las Vegas are spending hundreds of millions of dollars in advertising while practically no one is educating the public and convincing people to take care of their teeth.

I would argue that dentistry is the most under-advertised service in American history. Consumers are bombarded with 6,000 advertising messages a day. As the largest single advertiser of general dentistry, 1-800-DENTIST spent more than $20 million in 2010. Budweiser® spent that on Super Bowl® Sunday. Pharmaceutical companies with products like Lipitor® spend an average of $200 million a year on advertising for a single drug—one you can't even walk into a store and buy without a prescription! People who would gladly spend thousands of dollars on chrome wheels for their car would never consider making their teeth bright and shiny. And the same guy who spends $5,000 on a built-in backyard barbecue grill won't spend a nickel on his own grille.

> "Your competitors are not other dentists; they are Sony, Mercedes-Benz and Las Vegas."

The reason for this is simple. There is no concentrated effort, no *organized* way that dentists are using to explain the benefits of ideal dentistry. And that isn't going to change in the near future. Dentists will continue to be primarily solo practitioners, small businessmen who cannot marshal a large, concerted marketing effort to inform the public. (You've seen it done in a cooperative way with the beef and milk boards, for example, but we're still waiting for it to happen in dentistry.) So it remains for the individual practices to find effective ways to explain to their patients, and whenever possible to the public at large, that taking care of their teeth can have a profound effect on their lives.

I don't discount the fact that there are *some* dentists taking your patients away. But this just illustrates that most dentists think that the only patients worth having are the patients who appreciate comprehensive dental care. I think the real opportunity lies with all the patients who avoid the dentist. There are tens of millions of avoiders out there, and their neglect is inuring to your benefit with each passing day.

The first step, once again, is mindset. I'll say it once more: *If you don't believe that $15,000 to $20,000 of restorative and cosmetic dentistry that a patient may need is one of the best investments they can make—is one of the best reasons to borrow money and spend it on themselves—then that is your biggest barrier to success.* You will not be able to win against your real competitors (Sony, Las Vegas, et al.) who are doing an excellent job every day of convincing people that money spent with them will change their lives for the better.

There are a number of ways to combat this problem. The first thing that has to change is the perception dentists have that advertising and marketing are unprofessional, and that "selling dentistry" is a bad thing. Remember, persuasion is often a necessary step when people don't have the same knowledge we do, and this basic human interaction is the essence of a dental practice. Wouldn't patients be better served if they did regular preventive care, accepted the best restorative materials and procedures, and eliminated their gum disease? Wouldn't it be great if people knew about the value of dental implants versus

dentures, the comfort of lasers and the benefits of proper occlusion in terms of sleep, headaches and energy levels? The truth
is, dentistry has never been more exciting, or had more to offer
than it does now. But people don't know about it. As I said
before, it's not just in your best interest from a business standpoint, it's also your professional responsibility to tell them.

There aren't too many dentists; there are too many non-patients.
You need the right mindset, and you need to understand the
consumer mindset. Understand that people aren't motivated
on their own to pursue their ideal mouth. Understand that
most people have the money, or can find it. They just don't appreciate the value, which brings me to the issue of cost.

COST VERSUS VALUE

My friend Dr. Louis Malcmacher, who is a practicing dentist
and a riveting lecturer, often asks his audiences, "Do your patients think your fees are too high?"

This question always elicits a resounding "Yes!" from the crowd.
"So why not raise your fees 5 percent?" he asks. "If they're going to complain anyway, why not at least make more profit?"
Brilliant. And it also illustrates a point about the public: They
don't know how to value dentistry.

Is cost really an issue for most patients? That's not what the
research shows. Of course, nobody starts out wanting to spend
money on dentistry, for one simple reason: They don't appreciate the value they are getting. If we don't value something, any

price is too high. Conversely, if we do value it, then most of the time we find the money.

A dentist recently told me about a cosmetic patient of his. She was a bartender, who, though quite beautiful, had a gnarly set of teeth. He *didn't* decide that because she was a bartender she couldn't afford it, which unfortunately is what many dentists would do. He told her exactly what she needed to have her ideal smile, and what it would cost. A year later she came back to his office and said, "My boyfriend told me that if getting a new smile was that important to me, then he would pay for it." People can find the money for things they value.

Many small business owners, including dentists, let the process of pricing control their business. But they misunderstand the psychology of the American consumer. If price were the major driving factor in the economy, then why does Nordstrom exist? (Or Rodeo Drive, The Magnificent Mile® or Fifth Avenue?) Simply because some people don't want to buy their clothes from a pile on a huge table at Costco®. And they want help. And they want to be able to return something easily when it's not right. And they want quality because it's a reflection of themselves and enhances their self-esteem. That's part of the value proposition to them, and they are willing to pay for it.

Also, if price were the major driving factor, how did Starbucks® take people from complaining about paying 50 cents for a cup of coffee to gladly paying three dollars? Simple: perceived value. Starbucks is a great example of masterful marketing overcoming price: They create an environment where people want to gather; they design a warm, inviting space and they provide an insane number of choices to the coffee consumer. If you calculated the possibilities from their menu, there are over 10,000 different variations of coffee drinks available at any Starbucks.

That's what good practice marketing can do. It can take a patient from complaining about the cost of a prophy to gladly paying for a full set of veneers. And you have the comfort of knowing it's one of the best long-term investments they can make. (There's that mindset point again!)

If you are running a low-cost practice, the situation is different. Cost is your driving message, not quality. But if not, don't allow cost to be your driver, because it only speaks to the fact that patients don't value your services enough to pay you what your time is worth.

Now some dentists complain about competition from "discount dentists." Let me just say, the most challenging and least loyal patient is one who came to you because you were the cheapest dentist. They either don't value their own health, or money supersedes any other consideration. They view dentistry as a commodity, and they look for the lowest bidder. It's going to take some time and some effective marketing to gradually turn this patient into someone who values their own dental health and the care you offer. In the long run, I believe every patient is worthwhile, and worth the effort, but this is why I'm wary of promoting discount offers in your advertising.

Here is the only discount I would offer: a "cash courtesy" for full payment up front, where you reduce the fee by 5 to 10 percent. This is just too beautiful to pass up, and it only means that from a practical standpoint you're willing to help the patient out if they commit and help your accounting out. How do you do this without having an impact on your profits? Simple: Have "full retail" fees and then reduce them at your discretion.

Remember when hardcover books were $19.95? Then Amazon.com® came along and started discounting them. The book publishers decided to just increase the price of a book and then discount it in every bookstore by 20 percent—cover price, plus a sticker for a discount. Books became like cars, where no one pays the list price. The fees that you offer on elective procedures are quite flexible, and most often dentists err on the side of too low.

So why do patients ask about cost? Because they don't know what else to ask. They have no way of assessing your clinical skills. When they call your office and ask questions like, "What does a root canal cost?" they are really just trying to determine if they can trust you. That means if you answer the question with a dollar amount, you're giving the wrong answer. You're being literal about the question. Look at the question behind the question. They are really asking, "Are you going to take care of me, and can I trust you to at least not overcharge me?"

The answer to a price question is not, "A root canal costs $1,100." Instead, it should be, "Every patient is different, but it sounds like something that the doctor would be very concerned about, and we'd like to get you in the office right away. Don't worry about the cost of it right now. Our fees are reasonable for the area, but I really think you'll like the care that this practice offers."

Let's face it, you can't do a diagnosis over the phone. How can you tell them what it would cost to treat them properly? Get them in the office and let them experience your brilliant professional (and comprehensive marketing) skills. Convince them that their condition is much more important to you than money. And get them in right away, while they have dentistry on their mind. It will give the impression that you have the kind of availability that they need, and they won't go back into procrastination mode. We all get too wrapped up in sticking to our appointment schedule—and you're not thinking retail when you do that.

Get them in, give them a tour—an experience of your practice—and start the *relationship*. If they go home without getting any work done, they'll think it's the best dental appointment they've ever had. And you probably shouldn't charge for the initial exam on a new patient, so they'll be even more excited. If they have an emergency need, take care of it. Otherwise, schedule time later.

Don't get hung up on cost, or get involved with quoting fees. When they really think about it, most people don't really want discount treatment done on any part of their body. Most people, over time and with the proper guidance, will appreciate how important their oral health is. And I'm telling you that most people will be glad to pay for it. It may be a long way from where you are in your practice, but I promise you that you can get there.

It begins with the important steps of understanding how the consumer perceives you, and then transforming that perception. We'll talk about that transformation in the next chapter.

CHAPTER 5

BECOMING A
LIFESTYLE
ENHANCER

Over the past 15 years, there has been a major trend emerging in the American economy.

It used to be that consumers' spending habits generally conformed to their income level. By observing their clothes, their cars, their vacations and their toys, you could easily identify their income stratum. However, in recent years this trend has turned itself inside out. Now you commonly see millionaires buying t-shirts at Walmart® or Porsche® drivers who live in $1,000-a-month apartments. How did this happen? It all comes down to lifestyle.

Here is the mega-trend in the current US economy: If a product or service enhances a person's lifestyle, they want the *best*. When it comes to something utilitarian, something that serves a basic need, they want the *cheapest*.

Take for example the difference between televisions and DVD players. People at every income level are buying high-definition TVs. They spend thousands of dollars, research which is the best and often finance the purchase. But most DVD players sold nowadays are still in the $50-$100 range. Why? Because they all give the same result. There isn't a reason in the world to buy a $500 DVD player. A $49 machine works exactly the same, so there's simply no reason to spend more. (And Blu-ray™ HD players will soon become just as cheap!)

People do the same thing with clothes. I go to Nordstrom for a suit, and then drive to Target® for the socks. Why? Because I don't need a $15 pair of socks! I want three pairs of socks for $10. They're usually hidden under the suit anyway, so as long as they match, who cares? Consumers follow this pattern over and over when it comes to their lifestyle choices. For things they don't consider important, things they consider utilitarian, they go for the cheapest they can possibly find.

> **"Most people don't see dentistry as a service that enhances their lifestyle."**

So how does this relate to dentistry? Simple: Most people view going to the dentist as utilitarian. They see dentistry as maintenance—a necessary, but potentially avoidable expense, which they try to minimize as much as possible—not as a service that enhances their lifestyle. We know that they are wrong. But if we are going to change their mindset, we first have to change every aspect of their experience.

This starts with deciding who you want to be. Are you a maintenance service provider, somebody who fills their cavities, cleans their teeth and gets them out of pain? Or do you want to be an *enhanced lifestyle provider*, someone who considerably improves their appearance, health and quality of life?

With veneers, implants, whitening, Invisalign® and the many other services you offer, you're capable of transforming your patients' lives. But it's up to you to get them to see you that way. Remember, half the population doesn't see a dentist on a regular basis—and I assure you that *they* don't see you as lifestyle-enhancing. But I can almost guarantee that half your existing patients don't see you as more than a maintenance service either; or worse, an emergency resource.

Don't agree? Run a report or two out of your software. How much pending treatment do you have? How long is your average recall within your patient base? What percentage of your patient base comes in less than once a year? Most practices have more than a year's worth of production pending, and sometimes as much as two years. Most practices have an average recall of 11 months, with less than half of their patients coming in once per year. Sound like you? If so, you're a maintenance service, my friend. Fortunately, this can be solved by changing the way your patients view your practice.

Remember the Walt Disney story? Well, similar transformations have occurred in dozens of industries, from things as simple as blue jeans or coffee to museums and surgical centers. And Disney® continues to expand on this concept. Those of you who went to Disney World® 20 years ago remember waiting in long lines, often in the hot sun, for the best rides. Now those lines weave through a visually appealing structure, where you can't see how long the line is, you're out of the sun and you're at least mildly entertained. And they didn't stop there. Now you can make a reservation to get in a shorter line later in the day, and go do something else in the park in the meantime.

This is the approach I'm advocating for dentistry. You can look at every aspect of your practice and add a marketing element, suddenly taking an experience that was once tedious (or worse, that increased patient anxiety), and making it pleasant. Ideally, it might even increase patients' awareness of what the practice offers and make them more likely to want your services.

In Chapter 2, I gave you a short list of elements in your practice that had a marketing aspect to them. But here is a longer list of the things that, in my mind, involve marketing. Most likely every single one of them is something you can improve upon.

- The smell of your office
- How your staff answers your phone
- Your hours
- Your patient intake forms
- Your technology
- How you collect money
- The shape of your reception desk
- Your scrubs
- Your music and videos (both in the lobby and chairside)
- Your practice name
- The languages you and your staff speak
- Your signage

- Your on-hold and voicemail messages
- Your wall colors
- Your ceilings
- Your lighting
- The size of your operatories
- How you administer anesthesia
- How you appoint
- How you ask for referrals
- Your wall decorations, including diplomas and training certificates
- Your gender

Ok, maybe you can't change your gender (except perhaps in extreme cases, which I don't recommend). But every other item on this list can be improved upon to transform your patients' perception of your dentistry.

The solution is right there for you. It starts with the mindset that money spent on dentistry is one of the best long-term investments a person can make (I will beat that drum throughout the book) and that every part of your practice can have a marketing aspect to it. I will be challenging you to examine what the experience of your practice truly is, moment by moment, room by room, treatment by treatment, from the first phone contact on. Some of it you may find dismaying. But don't despair. It's all fixable. Most of it quite easily.

To begin this process, I want to help you get into the heads of your potential patients a bit more deeply and discuss the quirky nature of human beings.

CHAPTER 6

HUMAN NATURE: IGNORE IT AT YOUR PERIL

People are weird. Their actions often defy logic.

I know women who use coupons at the market because it saves them a dollar, but then spend $400 on a pair of shoes. I know men who come back from Home Depot® with tools that they will never figure out how to use. People who wouldn't buy a car without air bags go skydiving, or even BASE jumping. Parents buy their kid a new BMW® when he turns 16 and are shocked when he gets a speeding ticket a week later. I could go on forever with these.

There is a line from one of my favorite old movies, *Harold and Maude*, where Maude explains that "consistency is not a human trait." So true. Human behavior is ruled by all sorts of irrational urges, and we ignore this fact at our peril in business. This is especially true in the dental business. I will drive this point home many times in this book: If you pretend that human nature isn't true, isn't a real driving force in everyday behavior, you do so to your extreme detriment. It would be great to imagine that everybody loves dentistry and everybody wants it. It's just not true.

These are some basic points about human nature that I have found to be absolutely true. First, *we value most what matters least, and we ignore what's most important.* Because of laziness, familiarity or other reasons, we do this all the time. We do it with our families and our friends. We'll forget our wife's birthday but never miss an episode of *American Idol.* We'll buy expensive cars and not have life insurance for our family. This is human nature, and it's particularly true with decisions about our health. If our bodies are chugging along, taking care of themselves, we tend to ignore them. We want to assume we're fairly invincible. Of course, rationally we know it's not true, but it's human nature to behave that way. The biggest cause of death for people who have had a heart bypass is that they stop taking the medication necessary to keep them alive. They want to believe they are all better, even though they have had open-heart surgery. They have a scar on their chest to remind them every day, and yet…

Here's why: Avoidance and denial are normal. They are essentially how we get through our day. If we sit around thinking all day about the next terrorist attack, or a stock market crash, or a drunk driver crossing the center line and killing us, we're not going to get through the day. We have to be in a certain amount of denial. We avoid facing certain realities. We avoid making the connection between eating and gaining weight, for example. And, with all the facts available, including what is written right on the pack, two million people *start* smoking in this country every year!

Dentistry is one of the easiest things to be in denial about, and one of the easiest things to avoid. Enamel is really strong. It can really take some neglect and abuse, and people have figured this out. They figured out that they can wait to see you. For nine months. Twelve months. Two years. Five years. People avoid going to the dentist simply because it's not fun, and they would rather have fun. I know doctors who smoke, and I know dentists who are three months behind on their own prophys. That's human nature. We neglect things. And dentistry is something that in people's minds costs them money. All they're getting is maintenance out of it, remember? It uses up their time. It's unpleasant, potentially painful and expensive. That's a pretty easy thing to avoid.

> "Dentistry is one of the easiest things to avoid."

The truth is, it's just not human nature to do the things that are necessarily good for us. I've already talked about the importance of selling your patients on dentistry. But let's talk about just what you're selling. It's something much more than just dental health. You're selling self-confidence, a better appearance, higher self-esteem. Those are great things to be able to offer! If there were only one thing I could give to my child, it would be self-confidence. You get to give that to people all the time. You get to help them look better, to smile comfortably and proudly, which directly contributes to their self-image, how they feel as they go out into the world, and how they're received in the world.

Face it. America is an appearance-based society. We can wish that weren't true, but just look at the magazine covers. Look at the TV shows. Look at everything. But the great thing is, you're helping people with their appearance while at the same time making them healthier. For your patients, a healthy, beautiful smile could lead to a better job or a new relationship. It's actually been proven that when people smile more, even without a reason, they feel better and live longer.[10] You are selling a better life, a happier life—and that's something you should want to shout from the rooftops!

It is truly an amazing thing to be able to open your appointment schedule every day and say, "Hey, we might change one of these people's lives today. Let's pick who it is." Most people's jobs are nothing like that. But this is what you and your staff get to do all the time. That's pretty satisfying. That's something to be proud of. That's something to be excited about. That's something to talk somebody into—changing their life!

Deep down, every dentist wishes patients would just ask what your dentistry can do for them. But the really successful dentists have accepted that this is not human nature. If you resist that fact, not only are you cheating yourself out of greater success and a better lifestyle; you're cheating your patients out of a better life because they don't understand it. They don't make that value connection because their human nature is being drawn in another direction. You know the truth. And you have the power to improve their lives. Tell them. Help them understand.

Next I want to delve into how dentists view their patients, and how that is in direct conflict with how potential patients view you.

ACTION ITEMS:

1. Run reports on your pending treatment and patient recall. Use them as benchmarks for improvement as you improve your marketing.

2. Get to the gym.

3. If you're a smoker, quit.

CHAPTER 7

THE CONFLICTING MINDSETS OF PATIENTS AND DENTISTS

Let's go back to the statistic that roughly 50 percent of the population doesn't have a dentist. How does that happen? Honestly, the only way this can be possible is if they believe that they don't need one. Here is the first thing to remember about these dental avoiders: They are different. They are not like your patients. They think differently than your patients think. Your patients love you, or at least they should. And they understand why taking care of their teeth is important, and trust your professional recommendations, or at least they should. This is the opposite of what dental avoiders think. This difference is a big challenge for dentists, and because they don't make the distinction between the two, they behave the same way towards both new and existing patients.

But why even bother with these people? Isn't it a lot more fun to have patients who love you and want to come in? Perhaps, but let's start right there—with something I call "The Myth of the High Dental IQ."

Almost every dentist I speak with wants patients with a high dental IQ—meaning the new patient already knows and appreciates everything a dentist has to offer. But is that where the opportunity is? (Look at Figure 4.)

Figure 4

DENTAL IQ CHART

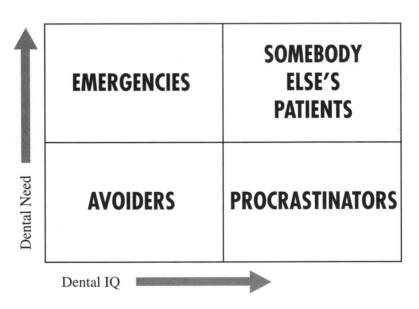

On the x-axis is Dental IQ, and on the y-axis is Dental Need. In the first quadrant are people who have a low dental IQ and a low dental need. They are the *avoiders*. They don't "need" a dentist. That is, they're not in pain, and they don't know why else they should go. Move along the IQ-axis and you have people who know better, but don't feel a strong need, like pain. These are the *procrastinators*. They at least know they should see a dentist, but they can't get around to it. Now move up the y-axis instead. People with a low dental IQ but a high need are *emergencies*. They've moved from avoidance to need, but they are more likely to ask for a Vicodin® than a root canal (they probably need both, so they're half right). The final quadrant has people with a higher dental IQ and a higher need. There is an important distinction here. These people have a higher need because they have a high dental IQ, not necessarily a dental problem. Because they believe that taking care of their teeth regularly is a health basic, it's a need for them. These people are called *dental patients*. In other words, they most likely already have a dentist.

This illustrates an important point. All the real opportunity is in the first three quadrants! Why is that? Because these patients are in some state of neglect, ready to learn what dentistry can do for them and why it can change their lives and their health. The only potential patients in the fourth quadrant are probably new movers, and though they may bring in their family, they are generally not in need of much more than basic care. If you know how to capture the patients in the other three quadrants, this is where the production is. And don't make assumptions about patients' ability to pay based on what quadrant they fall into. It's just as often about fear of pain as it is about fear of cost.

Let me digress for a moment here. Within most dental practices the patients usually fall into three categories. They are:

- the loyal few (10 percent)
- the satisfied many (60 percent)
- the reluctant maintainers (30 percent)

You know the three types. You may not know what the ratios of them are in your practice, but if you and your staff were honest about it, the percentages above would probably mirror your practice pretty closely. Obviously the goal is to move most of them into the first category.

My company offers an internal marketing and digital communication program called PatientActivator®. It is a comprehensive service that sends automated communications to your patients—appointment reminders, birthday greetings, email marketing campaigns and newsletters. Basically, the program pulls patient data directly out of your software and takes away a lot of the work for your front desk. (See Appendix I for more details.) But the first thing we do is take that data and analyze several factors about your practice: your average recall, how many patients are truly active, how many email addresses you have, how many cell phone numbers (and later I'll tell you why these are so important), and how many people have moved away.

One of the first things we learned when we started doing this analysis surprised me. I mentioned this statistic in the last chapter: For most of the practices, which are generally successful and well-run, the average recall was 11 months. Even more remarkable, this was the recall for what we categorized as active patients, which we liberally described as having been in the office at least once in the past three years. 11 months! That's sure not six. Practice managers I've spoken with around the country verify that this recall number is typical. Just imagine how much basic hygiene revenue is being missed in the average practice. Never mind how much more dentistry could have been presented if they only came in more often. This means that a large percentage of patients who have a dentist are essentially supervised avoiders. If you did the action item in the last chapter and ran the report, I believe you'd be shocked and dismayed yourself. But don't panic yet. This just spells opportunity. Marketing can solve this problem.

Think about the avoidance and denial that's going on even in the average good practice. This is human nature hard at work. Let's expand our ranking of your patients. Visualize your patients' dental IQ as a sliding scale:

- Total avoiders (unsupervised neglect)
- Emergency-only patients
- Casual about recall (supervised avoiders)
- Aware of comprehensive care, but not accepting
- Regular on recall
- Accepting and maintaining comprehensive care

Try to fit your existing patients into this spectrum, and I'll bet less than half are in the highest category—I'll bet less than 20 percent, in fact—and though many of them are in supervised neglect, it's a whole lot better than unsupervised neglect. This is why marketing is necessary, and everything in this book is about moving them up this scale, step by step. Keep in mind, these are the patients within your practice. Now let's consider the behavior of the non-patient.

PART ONE:
THE MINDSET OF THE NON-PATIENT

Let's examine what the segment of the population without a regular dentist is thinking. These avoiders and procrastinators, like the people who call 1-800-DENTIST every day, have a very specific set of beliefs. Or rather, they have rationalizations. They sound like this:

"I haven't had a cavity in years."

How many times do we hear something like that? No one has explained to them that in adulthood, their major problem is going to be periodontal disease, not simply tooth decay. Their understanding of why you see a dentist is to get rid of the cavities that they've generated with the 10 liters of Coke® they drink a week. And of course, they're self-diagnosing based on their last dental appointment years ago (they didn't have a cavity then, so they believe they're "cured").

"That visit-every-six-months thing was made up by the ADA."

People think this is just a money-making scheme or some old wives' tale that doesn't relate to their personal dental health in any way. As we know, it really should be more like three to six months, but we can't even convince them that they should be seeing a dentist at all. Some people should be going a lot more often, but they don't even believe in a basic level of preventive care.

"When it hurts, then I'll go."

That's their rule for taking care of their teeth—pain is the indicator of dental need. We know what that pain really means. It means they've waited too long, and they're going to need to spend some money (and they're not going to like that news). They don't understand that maintenance prevents pain, prevents tissue loss and keeps them a lot healthier. It never enters their consciousness.

"1 brush and floss; that should be enough."

That's if they even floss. How many of your patients floss every day? Most of them think, "I brush every day. That's enough." And who's helping them think that? The toothpaste companies. They have companies like Crest®, with their Pro-Health® toothpaste, and TV commercials saying, "It feels like I just came from the dentist!" (What, it makes your lips numb?) The subtext of these commercials, the subliminal message, is very important.

Now, I've worked for big ad agencies. I can picture the strategy session for this Crest campaign. A bunch of creative people sat in a room and said, "What do people really want from our toothpaste?" Then one guy said, "They want to never have to go to the dentist." So they all thought, "Well, let's create advertising that makes people think that without actually saying it." Because remember what they used to say? "See a dentist regularly." They don't say that anymore, do they? It's too competitive out there to promote you *and* their toothpaste, so they've eliminated *you* from the message. And they've gone way beyond that. They've created the fantasy impression that you can be eliminated altogether. Believe me when I tell you that consumers are dreaming of the day when someone tells them, "This toothpaste will keep you out of the dental office for the rest of your life." That toothpaste is a long way away, but the desire to stay away from the dentist forever is so strong that if a toothpaste company even hints at it, they've grabbed a toothpaste customer and turned them into a dental avoider.

"How could I possibly need this much dentistry? My teeth are fine."

This happens a lot when someone finally sees a dentist, briefly, and finds out just how much neglect is going on. But they're not in pain. So they finally start flossing and never go back. They've been presented with all this dentistry, and don't think they need it. They think, "You just want my money." Denial is a powerful thing.

Now, this is partially the fault of dentists. Some dentists present too quickly with a patient who's been avoiding. They have a patient who hasn't been to the dentist in 10 years, and they'll sit down after FMX and an exam, and say, "You need $9,000 of dental work done." This is in the first appointment. And they'll make it seem like it has to be done immediately. It's probably true because the patient has been neglecting for so long and he is probably in a certain amount of discomfort, but he's just not ready to believe it. He can't believe that today was the last day that he could afford to neglect his teeth.

So the patient doesn't believe the dentist, because the dentist hasn't established any credibility for why so much dentistry is necessary. Face it—it's not good news. Most people can go right into denial pretty easily on bad news like that, and they rationalize it. The avoidance technique is, "This dentist just wants a new boat. I don't need this." Now the truth is, they probably don't really have to start the treatment right then. They're not likely to die. But dentists have been told by more than one clinical lecturer that if they don't tell the patient everything they need right out of the gate, then they are not being professional.

Let's get real here. Enamel is tough, and so is the human immune system. Will your recommended treatment make a drastic difference in their life? Probably, but you can't get them to leap all the way over from avoidance to comprehensive acceptance in one conversation, unless you are one silver-tongued devil. And let's not forget the psychological factors. First of all, they have budgeted absolutely nothing toward dentistry—not this year, not last year, not next year. The idea of suddenly having that expense is shocking, and denial is the safe way out. If they don't have the money, it's a lot easier to say, "Well, I simply can't afford that. It will have to wait," rather than, "Hey, I'd better figure out how to get that money right now."

Knowing what patients think is an important step in moving them from avoidance and toward accepting treatment. But by itself, it's not enough. We also need to know the emotional drivers of this behavior.

REASON #1: THEY'RE AFRAID.

It's nothing more complicated than that. They have deep-seated impressions, usually from childhood, about a dental office. I've observed that most fearful patients either at one point had a really great dentist who passed away or retired, or a really bad one who's still practicing. But either way, their experience of dentistry was usually highly negative. When you're young, those experiences of fear and pain are heightened—so they make a much deeper impression and last a lot longer. Tension and apprehension only make the experience worse.

People carry this childhood impression through into their adult lives, and the memory is seldom associated with anything positive. (They don't walk around saying, "I hated the dentist, but at least all my teeth are healthy!") They're not motivated to go, and they're not going to admit to their fear. And it doesn't help that every entertainment medium out there is reinforcing the negative aspects of dentistry. Every few years a new movie comes out accentuating the horrific possibilities in dentistry or a survey shows up in *USA Today*® about how people would rather do their income taxes than visit the dentist. Counterproductive, to say the least.

When you practice dentistry every day, it's very easy to forget how scary it can be for people. Also, keep in mind that dentistry puts people in an unusual, vulnerable position physically. They are lying on their backs in a dental chair, letting a stranger stick his hands in their mouth. There aren't many other experiences like that—certainly not in my average week. Don't lose touch with that.

REASON #2: THEY DON'T TRUST YOU.

Don't take it personally. Potential patients have no relationship with you—no positive associations with your profession—and they have allocated no money towards this type of care. Remember, most people are either getting their medical care covered by insurance, or walking into a county hospital to get free treatment. They don't need a health care budget. Suddenly they need a dental care budget. Even with dental insurance, they will need an annual dental budget for the rest of their lives, because the coverage will be insufficient 90 percent of the time—particularly with regard to optimum comprehensive care. Know that part of your professional obligation is to address these issues head on. Trust is something built gradually, with a series of actions. This, again, is where marketing can help.

REASON #3: THEY DON'T SEE THE UPSIDE OF DENTISTRY.

These potential patients don't see the point in proactively taking care of their teeth. Nobody has explained it to them. And equally critical, they don't understand the cumulative effects of long-term neglect. If they don't have cavities, they think they're fine. If their gums are bleeding a little bit, they don't think it's a serious symptom. If they can't get rid of their bad breath, they just buy more Tic Tacs® and Listerine®. They don't understand what this neglect is inevitably leading toward. Why? Because no one has effectively educated them. I say *effectively* because someone may have told them something about oral health, but real education only happens when someone learns something, not when they just hear it.

In many cases, no one has even told people what they can expect from neglect. They make no connection between their minor tooth issues now and their grandfather who started wearing dentures in his fifties. It's human nature. Someone has to make that connection for them. And it's not the ADA. It's not their MD. It's not their mama. It's you.

PART TWO:
THE MINDSET OF THE DENTIST

As a dentist you have your own mindset, and believe it or not, some of these assumptions also come from avoidance and denial. I call these various thoughts "Fantasy Beliefs."

FANTASY BELIEF #1: "MY PATIENTS LOVE ME."

Probably fairly true. But the problem starts when you go on to think, "They love me, therefore they should want everything I have to offer them and intuitively know what those things are." Do you see any problem with that thought process? Is that anything like how people really behave? I'm sure most of your patients do at least like you or they wouldn't come in, but here's my experience: When patients say, "I really love my dentist," 9 times out of 10, they mean they love the staff (and if it's a male, it usually means either the dentist is cute or she has a cute hygienist). And even if they do love you, they don't necessarily know what you do. They don't necessarily understand why they should see you regularly or know everything that you can do for them.

This comes down once again to denying human nature. Dentists tend to think, "My patients should want to take care of their teeth." Right. And they should go to the gym, and eat right, and get regular physicals and limit their alcohol consumption. They should always send "thank you" notes and stop gambling in Vegas when they're winning. But they don't. This gets worse when the dentist expands this belief to new patients. He imagines that because (most of) his patients love him, new ones do too—automatically, without any time to build a relationship. Just like real life, right? Sure.

And something else is going on here, too. A little avoidance mechanism on the dentist's part—that little voice that says, "I don't want to have to sell. I don't want to have to promote myself. I don't want to have to convince anybody of anything. I want them to ask me for what's best for them and figure out how to get the money to pay for it on their own." This type of denial—typical in all of us—is unproductive, and will have a serious effect on your gross.

REALITY CHECK: What's your case acceptance? 30 percent? 40? That's how to measure how deep the love goes.

FANTASY BELIEF #2: "I SHOULDN'T HAVE TO ADVERTISE. MY DENTISTRY IS GREAT."

The history of capitalism is littered with companies who created great products and then disappeared because they couldn't figure out how to tell the world what they had. Or worse, they didn't think they actually needed to tell the world. "If you build it, they will come," is a great quote from a great movie, but it doesn't have much to do with real-world commerce. Sure, there was a time in dentistry when advertising was not only unnecessary, but illegal—and back then, all you had to do was put up a sign and your practice would fill up. That was a long, long time ago. Let it go. Enter the 21st century.

It would be nice if practices just grew on their own because everyone saw the value in taking care of their teeth, but they don't. The only way you can communicate with the non-patients is by advertising. You have to get out to the people who don't come through your door and tell them why they should want to come to you.

Advertising is necessary for two reasons: First, as I've mentioned before, you have stiff competition for their discretionary spending (which is the money left over after food, gas, car and housing expenses). Second, they have virtually no way of selecting you out of the hundreds of possible dentists. Dentistry is a parity service, remember? Here's another little tidbit about human nature: When we have too many choices, we don't choose.

REALITY CHECK: When you consider that the average American sees 6,000 ad messages a day, how can they know anything about dentistry? (When Budweiser spends more on one brand of beer than all of dentistry spends in advertising, it's just not possible. Plus, dentistry isn't quite as much fun as drinking beer with your friends.) People also don't know how much dentistry has changed, and how much has been learned about the connection between oral health and overall health. Advertising is where it starts.

FANTASY BELIEF #3: "EMERGENCY PATIENTS ARE ALL DRUG ADDICTS OR BROKE."

About 20 percent of the calls we get at 1-800-DENTIST are emergencies. Remember who they are—low dental IQ and high need. Pain is the motivator that told them they have a need to take care of their teeth, and nothing else matters to them before that. If they see a little plaque or they can't fit floss between their teeth (or their gums bleed when they do), that doesn't mean anything to them. Pain is what drives them. And what do we all do for pain? Take drugs. It may be Advil® or it may be Vicodin. But either way, we're looking for something to make the pain go away. That doesn't make someone a drug addict, it just makes them a person who wants to avoid pain. Big difference.

Now, of course people who are addicted to pain killers are going to call you too, but they're not going to be satisfied when you say, "I'll call in a prescription for two tablets." They'll say, "I'll need 20 to get me through the weekend." There's your indicator of a drug addict. But the successful dentists I know treat emergency patients all the time because they understand that if you take a neglecter or an avoider who's in pain and give them a positive experience of dentistry, you can create a patient for life.

"You create a loyal patient by giving them a transformational experience."

You create a loyal patient by giving them a transformational experience about something that they didn't even understand. You have the perfect opportunity to make the connection between their mouth and their body and their happiness and turn them into a lifelong patient. And that's the name of the game.

Now are emergency patients really broke? Here's how to find out. When they call after hours with an emergency, simply communicate to them that you expect to be paid at the time of service for the emergency visit. So, when the emergency call comes in (and inevitably it's Saturday night at 11, right?), just say, "I will be happy to meet you at the office. I do have a $300 emergency exam fee, so please be sure to bring that with you. We accept cash, Visa® and MasterCard®." If they really have a problem that can't wait until Monday, they'll show up ready to pay.

Not only does this ensure your patient has money, it's a great baseline relationship to start. They realize that they have to pay you for your services. How unique! So many patients don't. They say, "Well, could you bill me? Then I'll pay you gradually if I still have money." That's not the relationship you want in your practice. But if you create a relationship where they value your time, the next step is to get them to value your professional recommendation. Bring them in for emergency treatment, and then make sure that they have an appointment to come back later to finish treating the immediate problem. Introduce them to the idea of restoring their mouth to complete health gradually by saying something like, "I'm going to take care of your immediate need, and then later we can talk about what else is going on in your mouth." Now you start them on the right track, toward comprehensive care.

The final argument I hear against emergencies is that they are not good patients. I counter with this: These people are the procrastinators, the avoiders. They haven't seen a dentist in years, sometimes many years. It's not necessarily because they can't afford it. They're afraid, or they don't see the value. Or they don't understand the gradual negative process happening in their mouths. In my mind, these neglecters are walking around with thousands of dollars of restorative dentistry waiting to be done. Invite them to your practice and show them what great dentistry is.

REALITY CHECK: What do you do for pain? I'll bet it involves taking some kind of pill. Emergency patients in pain are no different.

How many hospitals have emergency rooms? All of them. Did you know that over 800,000 emergency room visits were due to "preventable dental conditions" in 2009 alone? That's an increase of 16 percent from 2006.[11]

FANTASY BELIEF #4: "ADVERTISING BRINGS IN TOO MANY SHOPPERS."

I hear dentists say this all the time, and it creates a negative mindset among their entire team. Sure, we all want patients asking for comprehensive treatment and offering to pay up front. But is that realistic? Maybe this has happened once or twice, and dentists are hoping for it to be a regular occurrence. Or maybe you have a friend who brags about it happening all the time—but if you need 100-200 new patients a year, how often is this really going to be the case?

The fact of the matter is we are all shoppers until we are buyers. This is a mistake small business people make all the time—they think they only have time for buyers. Imagine a jewelry store that had a big sign that said, "*No shoppers, only buyers,*" with a bulky security guard at the door to establish that you are ready to buy something before he lets you in. How long would that jewelry store be open?

We all act like shoppers, even when we are intending to buy. When you walk into a clothing store, with the full intention of buying something, you tell the clerk, "I'm just looking." Don't hate shoppers. They are us. It is just normal human behavior, and to a degree you have to prepare for it—and to a degree you have to ignore it.

Car dealerships, for example, know that when somebody walks into a dealership and says, "I'm not here to buy today," 50 percent of the time, they will leave with a car that day. Fifty percent! So what do you think the salesman hears when somebody indicates they're a shopper? They hear absolutely nothing. They don't even listen because they know it doesn't matter. It has nothing to do with that person's real intentions. It's normal behavior to say, "I am not a buyer," because you know what? They're not yet. They're shopping. They're looking. *A shopper is a buyer waiting for certain things to happen.* The right marketing makes those things happen.

Please remember, potential new patients can get dentistry anywhere. They are truly shoppers until the moment they accept treatment. A new patient who comes in for a cleaning and exam and never comes back is a shopper who didn't really decide to buy. Don't hate them for it—counteract it with good marketing.

If you recall, I mentioned a study we did in conjunction with Harvard University to understand people's behavior toward going to the dentist—a probe into the patient mindset, if you will—that revealed that people have as much apprehension about finding a new dentist as they have about actually going.

Those results helped us understand why 1-800-DENTIST was so successful. We realized people essentially wanted to talk to someone about the dentist before they talked to the dentist. In other words, they were shopping.

Recently I was listening in as one of my operators at 1-800-DENTIST spoke with a caller. The woman on the phone had been driving around her new neighborhood trying to pick a dentist based on how the office looked from the outside. This is how lost most people are when it comes to finding a dentist. When the operator found her an office, she said, "Oh, I was just there. It was a nice office, but when I went up to the door, it was locked—and even though I could see someone inside, they wouldn't come to the door."

My operator called the office and sure enough, they were closed for the holidays, and wouldn't even come to the door for a new patient! It blows my mind how successfully repellent some practices can be when it comes to new patients. But I was also reminded by that woman driving around looking at dentist signs that people have an incredibly hard time picking a dentist. This person was shopping in her car for a dentist, clueless about how to choose one except by the outward appearance of the practice.

There is a simple reason for this: Patients have no way to assess your clinical skills. There's no way to really know ahead of time if you're a really caring and skillful dentist or if you're not. A dentist friend of mine summed it up well, saying, "They won't know if I'm a good or bad dentist for 10 years." It reminds me of the George Carlin joke, that somewhere out there is the worst doctor in America—and somebody has an appointment with him tomorrow morning. That's the reality for people. They just don't know how to find a dentist or assess in any way how they're going to be treated. Which also means it's a great opportunity for you and your team. If you can allay that apprehension first on the phone and then with every step, from introducing them to the office to presenting and treating them, you've given them a transformational experience.

REALITY CHECK: Patients can't measure quality of clinical care, but they can measure quality of experience. The experience is what makes them loyal—and the experience is what makes them refer. You can focus on becoming a better clinical dentist all year long, but if you don't enhance the patient experience, you are going to lose a lot of shoppers along the way.

With these insights into how consumers think about dentistry, in the next chapter we'll explore why patients leave a dental practice.

ACTION ITEMS

1. Check your fantasy beliefs. Make a decision to replace them one by one with realities of human nature, and watch the results in how people respond to you.

2. Learn to love shoppers. Change how your staff views them.

CHAPTER 8

WHY PATIENTS
LEAVE

A very hard-working dentist I've known for years once said to me, "I don't get it. I get plenty of new patients every month, and I'm working hard. Why isn't my practice any bigger?"

Because I know his practice, I answered, "Your back door is bigger than your front door."

Realizing, after a moment, that I was not speaking architecturally, he asked how I knew that. I told him, "Let's run a report on your recall, and see how stretched out it is, and how many patients haven't been back in years." The stats were brutal. He had literally hundreds of patients who had not been in for years—and he thought they were active patients. My friend is not alone. Most dentists are concerned about how many new patients are coming in the front door, but not focused at all on the patients who are leaving the practice or the reasons why. I'm hoping by this point that you have run this report for yourself, and have a sense of what your true patient situation is.

After talking with hundreds of practices and interacting with thousands of potential patients over the years, here are the major reasons I've found why practices lose patients.

REASON #1: THEY MOVE AWAY.

People in this country move all the time. The national mobility factor (the percentage of people who change their address each year) is 16 percent. More importantly, 8 percent move out of their current county, and 8 million people move out of state every year[12]—which means they are probably not going to go to the same dentist. That means if you live in a city like San Francisco, you can expect to lose 8-10 percent of your patients every year. Do you even know when that happens? Most likely you only find out if the patient asks for dental records, or if an appointment reminder comes back with an "addressee unknown" stamp. What are you doing to stem that ebb tide?

REASON #2: YOUR PRACTICE DOESN'T OFFER WHAT THEY WANT.

They've heard about Invisalign, or no-prep veneers, or lasers, or same-day restorations with CEREC, or they saw a news special on conscious sedation, and you don't offer these things. Or they saw an ad for Zoom!® and you don't do Zoom!—or worse, you don't offer in-office whitening at all. So they go somewhere else to get it. They like the new office and its advanced technology, and you never hear from them again.

REASON #3: THEY DON'T KNOW WHAT YOU DO.

I can't tell you how many times I've heard a dentist say that he had an existing patient suddenly come into the office with new veneers. "When did you do this?" he'll ask incredulously. The patient will excitedly explain that they saw an ad for a great "cosmetic" dentist—not a crown-and-bridge journeyman like the patient believes *he* is—who did a wonderful job creating their beautiful new smile. Then the dentist explains that he does veneers also—just a little too late.

You may have a laser. You may have done hundreds of hours of CE to become an AGD Fellow. You may offer IV sedation, Zoom! and Invisalign, but believe me, your patients don't know that. Maybe you think that you or your team have told them once, but you're not sure. Or maybe you assume they know because you have a brochure in your office. The reality is, your patients spend most of the time in your office looking at the ceiling, so unless it's written there, they haven't read about it, and they probably don't know you offer it.

> **"Telling people what you do only once is not effective marketing."**

This leads to an even bigger issue that is at the heart of marketing a practice—*telling people what you do only once is not effective marketing*. They usually are only listening if it's something that matters to them right at that moment. Effective practice marketing means telling your patients over and over all the services your practice offers, and explaining the benefits of those services. Communicate to your patients, repeatedly, what you do. It's your greatest resource for increased production.

REASON #4: THEY THINK YOU'RE TOO EXPENSIVE.

This means they don't value what you do. It also means that no one is building up the value of your dentistry in their minds— not you, not your team, not your office environment. They just get a bill. One of the most common complaints we get at 1-800-DENTIST is about dentists' fees. It's not because our members charge more than anyone else. It's because people don't understand what good quality dentistry costs. They'll say, "He charged me $1,000 for a root canal!" Once we explain that that is the going rate in Seattle, or wherever, they generally calm down. They just didn't want to be taken advantage of and never had the fee explained to them.

> "Most people don't understand what good quality dentistry costs."

This is one of the main reasons people avoid the dentist in the first place. They think it's expensive ("And insurance doesn't pay for it," they lament!) and all they're paying for is discomfort. In order to bring patients into comprehensive care, they have to appreciate the value of what you do. This means your team, your office environment, your technology and you yourself have to communicate to the patient why they should value the care you provide.

REASON #5: THEIR INSURANCE CHANGED, AND YOU DON'T ACCEPT IT.

Not much you can do about that, right? There might be. At 1-800-DENTIST we ask them if they are willing to go out of network for the right dentist, and very often, in fact more than half the time, they will. Most people want good dentistry, not necessarily the cheapest. Let your patients who are leaving because they have been switched to a closed plan know that you would still be happy to treat them, and hope they would find value in the relationship. A surprising number will stay. Others will come back when they don't like the care they get somewhere else. But none of these patients will stay with you if you don't ask.

Here is something very important to remember when a patient leaves you because their insurance changed: You have to let them know that you understand that cost is a factor, and that you are more than happy to send their records to their new dentist. But then tell them two more things: First, any time they have questions about what the other dentist is recommending for treatment, you are always happy to answer those questions at no charge. The second is even more critical: Let them know that they are always welcome to come back to the practice. Otherwise, many patients who leave you are too embarrassed to come back (even though they miss the care you gave them) because in their mind they left you because they were cheapskates. If they understand that you do appreciate their need to consider costs, and that they can always come back to you, many more will return if their coverage changes again or if they simply miss the level of care you provided.

REASON #6: THEY ARE EMBARRASSED ABOUT HOW LONG THEY'VE PUT OFF THEIR RECALL.

This may seem strange, but people feel uncomfortable about being chided for neglecting their exams and cleanings. With some people, it gets to a point where they are more comfortable seeing a different dentist. Don't make your patients feel guilty. I know many a hygienist who will not so gently scold the patient about how long it's been since the last appointment. They don't need that. Don't let your appointment coordinators do it either. Let the patient know you're there when they are ready, and ask how you can make it more convenient for them. Do they want to schedule the appointment six months out, just to get it in their calendar? Do they need a special time of day? Find out. Don't judge them, just help them keep their teeth as a priority.

At 1-800-DENTIST, we train our operators to be two things: compassionate and non-judgmental. These are the same qualities you should want in your own team.

REASON #7: THEY DON'T BELIEVE YOU CARE.

What I mean is, they don't think you care about them *personally*. It's very easy for dentists to get caught up in the clinical side of what they're doing, and not inform the patient. Very often the staff is multi-tasking and doesn't pay proper attention to the patient, but it only takes a moment to let that person know that you understand what's going on with them—their fear, their discomfort—and suddenly they feel cared for. They don't expect dentistry to feel good, which is all the more reason to take the time to acknowledge what they might be going through. Otherwise you're communicating that all they represent to you is income. Trust me, they don't like feeling that way.

Here's the interesting part: Every single one of these reasons why patients leave is within your control, with the exception of patients moving away. Most often, the simple solution is good communication—the kind of interaction that shows patients that they are in a relationship with you that benefits their life-long oral health. Show them you care, relate to them, equip your office with the latest technology and for goodness sake, tell them what you do.

Getting new patients is tough enough. It's worth the effort to keep them. Part of that is understanding what patients want most from you. That's what the next chapter is about.

ACTION ITEMS

1. Run a report on how many patients haven't been to your practice in over two years. Deactivate patient records of people you know have moved away.

2. Check your guilt trips at the door. Make it part of the morning huddle to remind your staff not to judge people because they've put off dentistry.

3. Ask every patient who is going to leave because their insurance changed if they are willing to stay, and explain that they are always welcome back.

CHAPTER 9

WHAT PATIENTS WANT MOST FROM A HEALTH CARE PROVIDER

What would drive the growth of your practice the most? Team efficiency? New technology? More CE? All those would certainly help, but would they *drive* your growth? No. The only thing that drives any business is knowing what your customers want most and finding a way to give it to them. Deciphering this is the main challenge for every business. So what do patients want *most*? Low fees? Whitening? The latest technology? IV sedation? Saturday hours?

I'll give it to you simply: none of the above. What they want is less tangible but almost universal when it comes to health care providers. Study after study shows the same thing. The number one thing patients want most is to feel that the doctor and his team care about them. They *expect* you to be well-educated, well-trained and well-equipped. That's baseline. (So you had better at least be those things!) But what matters most is their perception that you care about them as an individual. The implicit lesson here is that the real driver for growth is patient perception, not quality of service.

Let me put it slightly differently, reiterating a point I've made before: Patients can't assess quality of care, but they can assess their own experience.

Patients might tell you something else is more important. They may even believe it. But put this theory to the test, and you'll discover that human nature prevails again. Pay attention to the patient experience, and I'm quite sure you'll notice the difference. Accept this fact: Everyone wants to feel important, and that the focus is completely on them. Create that feeling for them, and you will drive your growth to amazing heights.

How do you achieve this? It boils down to very simple, very powerful actions: genuine empathy, effective communication and listening.

To illustrate this point, let me tell you about a study that was done regarding surgeons and malpractice suits.[13] The purpose of the study was to determine if surgeons were sued more or less often depending on their communication skills, and it involved audio taping the doctors as they talked with their patients. The first interesting find was that there was no strong correlation between a surgeon's level of competence and the numbers of suits filed against them (except that more highly skilled surgeons tended to be sued *more often* than less competent ones). However, the most revealing part of the study was that surgeons who were sued significantly less talked to their patients for an average of three minutes longer during the consultation. It wasn't just the time, though. They also tended to ask questions like, "Do you understand the procedure? Do you have any questions? Are you comfortable with what's going to be happening?" In essence, what they were saying is, "I care about *you*." This also explains why the more skilled (and perhaps more arrogant?) surgeons got sued more.

Another study showed that a good percentage of medical litigation could have been eliminated by a simple apology by the practitioner.[14] Now, I'm not saying don't be good at what you do. Be good, too. But the way to truly distinguish yourself—the way to generate loyalty—is to let patients know you care. And it's easy. It takes so little time. It just takes a little mindset change on your part, and realizing,

"Patients can't assess quality, but they can assess experience."

"Oh, yes, what I do is not always fun for the patient, but it can have a profound effect on their life, so I need to help them through the process." You do that and they'll be loyal. They'll never leave. They'll refer to you. They'll accept treatment more readily and will be much more compliant with recall.

I'll give you a perfect example. I happened to be in a member dentist's office one morning, and he was having a bit of a crisis. The day before, a new patient had come in for whitening and gotten halfway through the procedure before mentioning that she was lactating. Sure enough, it was on her intake form, but they had missed it. They stopped the procedure immediately and explained why to the patient. She went home and told her husband, who called the next morning and demanded to know why they had done the procedure when they knew they shouldn't have.

The dentist was sitting there trying to decide what to do. He told me he had called his insurance carrier who told him that he should have known better (very helpful!). He talked to his attorney who said not to talk to the husband, or anyone else, about this any further. Then he called the whitening manufacturer, who assured him that although it wasn't recommended, there was no contra-indication for lactating women. (The safest choice is simply not to recommend *anything* to pregnant or lactating women.) They said no studies had been done either way, but with the barriers used on the procedure, the woman would have had much more exposure if she had used over-the-counter whitening strips.

He also called an Ob-Gyn friend of his, who told him that to her knowledge there was no risk. Now, as an aside, you should know that this dentist has a fabulous practice, a beautiful office that also offers a number of spa procedures such as facials and skin treatments. He thought he should probably follow his lawyer's advice, but he also thought he should call the husband back. He didn't know what to do.

He asked what I thought, and this is what I told him: "Call the husband immediately and explain everything that you have found out from the whitening company and the Ob-Gyn. Tell him you believe his wife is at no risk whatsoever, but if he has any doubts to please consult with his pediatrician, and whatever else he needs to do to be comfortable. Please do it and just send us a bill."

Though he was nervous, he called the husband and explained everything very thoroughly. He didn't know what the eventual outcome would be, but he felt better about his choice.

The next day, the husband came in himself *to get a facial,* of all things, saying, "My wife has been raving about this place all day, and I just had to come here myself and see what it was like."

So not only did the dentist diffuse a bomb by *not* doing what his lawyer told him, which was to not speak to them ever again, he communicated this message: "I care more about what happens to your wife than what my lawyer or your lawyer is going to say or do. Our concern is about your wife and possibly your child. Let's take care of that." And he communicated that sentiment so effectively that now he has two loyal patients instead of one lawsuit.

It comes down to this—you may have heard it before, but it's health care in a nutshell: *People don't care how much you know until they know how much you care.* Your level of expertise is secondary to you actually caring about them as human beings because they are all different; they all are individuals with individual needs, and they want to be treated that way. And while ignoring your attorney's advice is not always a good idea, letting patients know that you care is.

Can you see the marketing power of expressing this genuine caring? The effect is profound, and this touches on one of the most important aspects of this book: building loyalty. In the next chapter I'll get much deeper into how that is accomplished.

ACTION ITEMS:

1. Analyze your internal policy on fixing mistakes.

2. Change it if necessary. Make sure it's empathetic and goes beyond their expectation. Every person in the office should know what it is and the thinking behind it. Most of all, give your team members permission to "be nice" on their own when dealing with disgruntled patients. Have apology gifts on hand. (More about those in Chapter 12.)

CHAPTER 10

MOVING BEYOND
PATIENT SATISFACTION

Businesses are constantly measuring "customer satisfaction." J.D. Power and Associates® has built a huge business based on it. Unfortunately, it's only useful to the companies as bragging rights.

Customer satisfaction is not the ultimate goal that companies should be striving for—and measuring it doesn't give them any indication of whether that person will buy another car from them, for example. This may not seem logical, but you won't be surprised when I tell you that it comes down to another quirk of human nature: When people are satisfied, it is because they got what they expected. "Wait," you're probably saying, "How can *satisfied* be a bad thing?" It's not *bad* (certainly not as bad as having an *unsatisfied* customer), but it doesn't mean they are loyal. Customer loyalty is the brass ring in business and in marketing—and you can have it in dentistry in spades.

In this modern age of hundreds of brand choices, customer loyalty is hard to come by in any industry. Airlines compete daily on price, restaurants are busy one year and closed the next, designers come in and out of fashion. But some companies maintain their customer base no matter what. You can see it in the success of their business. Southwest Airlines® is profitable when other airlines are cutting services or filing Chapter 11. Toyota® raises their prices each year while GM® and Chrysler® offered their employee discount to everyone in America and still had to beg for bailouts by the federal government. Apple® is now the number one selling laptop computer, while costing significantly more than the equivalent PC laptop, feature for feature. Why is that? The answer is loyalty.

What is the key to loyalty? It's right there in the definition of a satisfied customer—they got what they expected. A loyal customer experienced something *unexpected*. This is where human nature comes in: The unexpected is what sticks in our minds. Generating loyalty comes down to what I call "The Law of the Memorable Moment." If you give people what they expect, your service won't stand out in their minds. If they get something more, something different, something better than they expected, they will remember. And they will become loyal.

I'm a loyal Southwest Airlines customer, for example. That's because the website is always easy to navigate, the prices are always good, there is a good selection of routes, always with short layovers, their frequent flier system is easy and not bogged down with crazy rules and the staff is *friendly*. Because of all that, I will go out of my way to use Southwest whenever possible.

I used to be loyal to American Airlines®. In fact, I have over 500,000 frequent flier miles saved up. But on the average flight they have *two seats* available for frequent fliers, and you often have to book a year in advance to use them. And every time I have to change an American flight, even with my Platinum status and even online, it's a $100 fee in addition to any change in the fare. On top of that, their flight attendants, once the gold standard of the industry, are often irritable, and even surly at times. There were times when I actually wanted to take the flight attendant's name down and write to American to inquire if this new rudeness was company policy. Maybe their salaries were reduced, maybe they cut back on crew size, but *I don't care! I'm trapped inside their aluminum tube for five hours and I want to be treated like a paying customer!*

> "The Law of the Memorable Moment: People remember the unexpected."

So what did American Airlines do? They made it easy for Southwest to give me something unexpected. My expectations kept getting lowered, and my satisfaction had turned to dissatisfaction. American sends me letters telling me that the frequent flier program requirements are getting stricter and I'll need more miles for the same type of flight. Southwest sends me a free luggage lock. American changes my main route of travel to include a three-hour layover. Southwest sends me free drink coupons. American cancels my flight as I wait to board. Southwest arrives 10 minutes early.

Southwest gives me one memorable, unexpected moment after another. Sure, flying is never a particularly pleasant experience, with security being so crowded, having to bring your own food, tight seating, etc. But that's what makes it such a great analogy. A dentist visit is not fun for most people—and I think that's fantastic. It means that there are countless opportunities to give them something unexpected.

Here's something else that's very important. Remember when I said dentistry is a parity service—that to most people, dentistry is the same at every office? This ties right in to loyalty, because when your product or service is perceived as essentially the same anywhere, the best thing that you can do is make the *experience* different. You can give them an experience of dentistry they won't believe they can get anywhere else. I'll describe in detail how to do this in Chapter 11, but first, let's take a look at your patient base, and see who's loyal and who isn't.

There are three very significant differences between a loyal patient and a satisfied one. The first "symptom" of a loyal patient is they are absolutely consistent in their recall. That's because there is a foundation of trust in your professional recommendations. They enjoy visiting your office and seeing your staff, and they believe in taking care of their teeth. Second, a loyal patient would never go to anyone else for their dentistry. They are locked into your practice until they move a thousand miles away or you retire. Third, and most importantly, they talk about you to people. They recommend you. They are your walking, talking billboards—town criers for your practice—because they see you as special and want people to know about it.

So that's the definition of a loyal patient:

1. They are consistent on recall and receptive to treatment;
2. They would never see another dentist;
3. They refer others to your practice.

Think about how many of your patients fit this definition. Now think about how much more you could do in your practice if you increased this percentage. Each day, as you see patients, ask yourself if they are loyal or just satisfied. If they're not loyal, this book is going to help you to change that. Here are a few quick tests you can do:

Test #1: Review your patient recall report. You might want to limit it to patients who have been in during the past 36 months, otherwise the real stragglers skew the numbers. This will give you a sense of how loyal your patients are, in that they believe you when you tell them they need to come in every four months or six months.

Test #2: What is your case acceptance? If it's below 50 percent, then your patients, on average, don't believe you.

Test #3: Think back: Has a long-time patient ever walked into your office with a full set of veneers that they had done somewhere else? Or gotten whitening at a BriteSmile® center? That's a sure indicator that your patient base isn't loyal.

One more point about loyalty—it matters as much, or more, in dentistry than many other businesses. That's because you are going to make your money over the lifetime relationship with your patient, not on the first visit. Many other businesses make all their money in the first or second purchase. That's not you. You want to be there with them from the first prophy to the last implant—tens of thousands of dollars. You also want all their friends and family to come to you. Loyalty means the difference between a $500,000 practice and a $2 million practice.

Loyalty doesn't just come from doing unexpected things right. It also comes from how you respond when things go wrong. A perfect example happened to me recently at my car dealership. I received a notice that my Infiniti had a recall on some minor part. I was told that it would take a few hours, so my assistant followed me to the dealership and I dropped the car off. At the end of the day, she dropped me off at the dealership, but when I tried to pick up my car, they told me that they didn't have the right part for my specific model—so the car wasn't ready.

I asked if they could give me the car back so I could bring it in some other day, but the service representative said, "No, the engine is all taken apart, so we just left it that way since the part will be here tomorrow."

At this point I was getting a little steamed. I asked why no one had called me. "We're sorry about that," he said. "We just realized that the part wasn't the correct one a little while ago."

Now I was fully irritated, partially at myself because I trusted them (and let myself get dropped off rather than having my assistant wait). Just as I was about to express my anger, something remarkable happened. The service manager came over and said, "Mr. Joyal, I heard about what's been going on with your car. And you know what? I'd be way more upset than you are right now if this had happened to me." I thought, "Well, I guess I could get more upset if I tried," but he had totally disarmed me by copping to the fact that this shouldn't have happened.

Then he said, "Let me tell you what we're going to do. I'm going to give you a car to take home. Take it to the office tomorrow, and when the repairs are done, I'm going to bring *your* car to your office and make the switch. Don't worry about anything. Just take the car, go, and we'll take care of it from here."

What did he do? He took me from irritated and disenchanted with Infiniti all the way to loyal by doing something completely unexpected in today's business world—he took responsibility, and he did everything possible to make it better. In so doing, he turned a negative situation into a positive one. Not to mention the fact that I tell people about this experience all the time—another sign of a loyal customer. Here's the other important aspect to consider: Had my car simply been fixed as expected, I would have been satisfied. I'd be a typical satisfied customer who got what he expected, with no real impression made either way about the dealership. It would have been positive, but not profound.

> **"Take responsibility, and do everything possible to make the situation better."**

This is the essential message of this story: You will make mistakes—sometimes big ones, and sometimes with your best patients—but it doesn't matter if you know how to handle the situation to create loyalty. People don't expect you to be perfect. But when things go wrong, they expect you to understand why they're not happy and make it right.

You can do this easily, and make it staff policy. The first step is to let the person know immediately that you understand what they are going through. Tell them how you are going to fix it, and make the solution as easy and convenient for them as possible. Have a system in place that your whole team understands for going the extra mile to make things right.

The amazing truth is that most people, most businesses and most dentists don't know how to do this, or why they should. This means that you have a fabulous opportunity to outdo the competition.

Some businesses are masters of this. Starbucks has a policy of remaking any drink over that's not perfect—and the few times I've asked them to, they've also given me a coupon for my next drink free. That's getting it.

I am also a big fan of Maui Jim® sunglasses. They have the best lenses in the business, in my mind. But even better, when something happens to a lens, like a crack from the tension on the frame (or me sitting on them!), I send them to Maui Jim. For the price of shipping, they send me back glasses with brand new lenses. No charge. I don't even have to send a copy of the purchase receipt. I have probably bought 20 pairs of Maui Jims over the years, and none of any other brand. Many business owners think that this kind of service is too expensive.

They're just plain wrong. It's cheaper. And these companies have the profits to prove it.

Here's another important business statistic: It is estimated that it costs six times more to get a new customer (patient) than it does to keep an existing one. *Six times.* It's always cheaper in the long run to keep a patient. Remember that story in the last chapter about the lactating patient? That was a classic case of doing something totally unexpected and turning both the husband and wife into loyal patients.

Can you think of a situation where you were a customer and everything was fine for years—until an employee did one thing wrong and didn't apologize for it, or the company didn't take care of it, and you were finished with them? You can probably think of several. And it's because you were merely a satisfied customer. You got what you expected—and then one day you didn't, and it was over. They had never done anything unexpected to earn your loyalty and they didn't know how to fix it when something went wrong.

You don't have to be perfect clinically (though it would be nice). I'm convinced that it's more important to the strength and longevity of your practice that you are doing the many non-clinical things that it takes to generate loyalty.

I emphasize loyalty in dentistry because of one very important thing—how valuable that long-term relationship is with the patient. In the next chapter, I'll show you how to calculate that value and apply it to your business.

ACTION ITEMS:

1. Look at your recall history report and your case acceptance percentages, and give yourself a gauge of how loyal you think your patient base is. Use them as benchmarks for improvement.

2. Do surveys of your patients about how they feel about the practice, and if anyone in particular did not treat them the way they wanted to be treated. Programs like PatientActivator do this automatically, so be sure to read the responses.

CHAPTER 11

THE TRUE VALUE
OF A NEW PATIENT

To understand why patient loyalty is so important, you need to fully appreciate the true, long-term value of a new patient.

Most big businesses track their marketing cost to attract a new customer very closely, and they know fairly precisely what revenue will be generated relative to that expense. In many small businesses this is also fairly clear. An ophthalmologist knows, for example, that he needs to spend $500 in advertising, on average, for every Lasik case. But he knows he will make $5,000 in revenue on that case. It's fairly straightforward. In dental practices, it's a little more difficult to measure, in part because you don't really know what the patient is going to spend when they first come into the office. For this reason, most dentists don't have any conscious sense of the value of a patient. So let's break it down.

What is the average time span that a patient remains a patient? Would you say, conservatively, 10 years? Now, what does the average patient spend over that time period? Let's say $500 a year, with some restorative and regular prophys. (You can use whatever average number you think is accurate for your practice, but I'd say $5,000 over 10 years is on the low side.)

Most dentists are looking at their advertising cost and measuring it against what the patient spends *in the first visit*. Why in the world would you do that? You'll most likely not do any major treatment on the patient for 18-36 months. Advertising expense has to be viewed against the long-term value of the patient.

Now here is the most important part of the calculation, and one that most dentists miss: If you are asking for referrals and giving that new patient a good dental experience, they are estimated to refer *five* new patients over the next five years. If each of those referrals spends $5,000, that's another $25,000—all because of that first new patient. Total lifetime value: $30,000.

Now, imagine how you can dial this number up by increasing patient loyalty, thereby increasing two numbers in the calculation—the level of case acceptance and the number of patients referred. Now that number really goes up. Which is why I believe that when you factor in whitening, cosmetic treatment and implants, $5,000 per patient is an extremely conservative average.

A letter we received recently illustrates this point very well. It is from a dentist who bought a practice from a 1-800-DENTIST member, but felt he couldn't afford the advertising expense, so he dropped the membership. This is what he wrote:

"This is a note to relate to you my experience with patients referred to this office through 1-800-DENTIST. Although I'm currently not a member of the service, it has impacted my practice in a most positive manner. I purchased my practice four years ago from a retiring dentist who had been an 11-year participant in the 1-800-DENTIST service. Unfortunately, very tight finances did not allow me to continue the previous doctor's membership. Now, four years later, while doing a referral analysis, I noted that my production for the past 12 months for patients referred by 1-800-DENTIST totaled $83,770 even though I have never directly received a 1-800-DENTIST referral. Needless to say, I'm now on a waiting list for my area to become a member of 1-800-DENTIST. I only wish I had been able to find a way to continue the service immediately after I purchased the practice." Steven Slotnik, DDS.

This is a clear demonstration of how the value of a new patient is long term, and that something extremely valuable is lost when you fail to get a new patient in. This is what Dr. Paul Homoly, a master of getting patients to accept treatment, calls "building the stacks." What he means is that bringing in new patients and creating a transformational experience lays the foundation for years of production in the future.

With this in mind, what should you be willing to spend to get a new patient? I would think that $200 in advertising or more would easily be worth the investment, if your case acceptance is good and your internal marketing is working up to par. Many dentists might think that number is too high—except those building fast-growing practices, who would pay that all day long for new patients. In fact, I've met dentists who, because of the city they're in, or the type of dentistry they're trying to attract, would and happily do pay twice that.

I think dentists often use the cheapest advertising cost they have ever experienced as the benchmark for what a new patient should cost. Perhaps they did a promotion that cost $800 and brought in 20 patients. Even though it was a once-in-a-lifetime situation—and they've never been able to replicate that cost in any other advertising—they still think that finding a new patient should cost $40. Not likely.

> "Creating a transformational experience lays the foundation for a lifetime of production."

Think about what a new patient is really worth to your practice, and be realistic about what it's worth to you to get more new patients. Then plan your advertising spending accordingly.

Now let's factor in something else very important: contribution margin. Remember that concept that I introduced to you in Chapter 3? Once your overhead is covered, new patients become even more valuable, because a much greater percentage of the revenue is now profit. And you can also afford to spend more on marketing to attract them. So if a new patient generates $5,000 in production, and your overhead is already accounted for, your expenses for treating that patient really only include labs, supplies and a portion of employee time. If that totals 30 percent of the fee I'd be surprised. So why wouldn't you spend $500 to get that patient, or even as much as $800? You're still making $2,700 in profit. On $5,000! When you do the math, it sounds crazy not to do this.

I reiterate the idea of contribution margin here for two reasons: First, you should always be aware of that number and aim to get past this threshold (you can figure out what it is just by calculating your fixed expenses for the year). Second, because once you get past this point, your profit margin is so significant that you can afford to allocate another 5 or even 10 percent of the extra profit to advertising. This is what will take your practice to an even higher level.

Okay, enough numbers. In the next section, we'll get into the nitty-gritty of making your marketing work through every aspect of your practice. As I said, a dental practice is a great environment for creating unexpected experiences. The next chapter is all about what you can do every day to generate loyal patients.

ACTION ITEMS:

1. Calculate your contribution margin threshold. Formulate a strategy to blast past it.

2. Tell all your staff the true value of a new patient, and keep reminding them of that value.

SECTION TWO:

REFINING
YOUR
MARKETING

CHAPTER 12

LOYALTY
MAGIC BULLETS

I sincerely hope that I've convinced you to move your patients from satisfied to loyal. I also hope you can see how this is what transitions you from being a general/generic dentist to a lifestyle enhancement provider. Thus far I've presented how patients and non-patients think and why patients leave. Now let's talk about how you get them to stay.

First, let me emphasize once again that there is a tremendous opportunity to create patient loyalty in this current environment, and here's why: Most businesses are awful at customer service and customer relations. The consumer's normal experience ranges somewhere between indifference and incompetence. In other words, opportunity is *pounding* at the door. You can distinguish yourself not only from other dentists, but from most other consumer experiences as well.

With dentistry, as I've said, the expectation is low. People are expecting to be uncomfortable. They're expecting to be in a health care environment, where physicians and hospitals have set a baseline that is generally uncaring, and sometimes horrific.

Let me reiterate the third aspect of a loyal patient from Chapter 10: *They tell other people about you.* This element is critical because advertising is expensive. (I know. I make my living at it.) But do you know what's inexpensive? Word-of-mouth patients—and that's what loyal patients will bring you. Notice I didn't say free. There should be an expense associated with getting word-of-mouth patients, usually in the form of rewarding the referring patient. If that sounds like a loyalty tip, it is. Now here are several more rock-solid, time-tested ideas that you can start applying tomorrow, and the reasoning behind them. Remember, though you may have heard many of them at one time or another, I want you to look at them now from a marketing perspective.

LOYALTY TIP #1: THANK PATIENTS FOR REFERRALS.

You should have a system where someone is being thanked for every word-of-mouth patient who came in. And I mean every single one. Not only is gratitude a key to a happy life and a strong business, it's also something people neglect constantly. Don't. Have a budget to reward referring patients. It can be a handwritten note, or movie tickets or a bottle of wine. Given the lifetime value of each new patient, this is no place to tighten the purse strings. If someone sent you a restorative or cosmetic case, step up with something memorable. You don't want to be remembered for being cheap or ungrateful.

I'm very fond of the handwritten note. Nobody writes letters anymore, and few send cards. This is your chance to do something unique. If a patient recommends someone to your practice, write them a handwritten note thanking them. And be specific: "Thanks so much for sending your sister-in-law Brenda to us. She's wonderful, and we're going to take good care of her. See you soon!"

That's powerful stuff, and it often means more than sending a gift.

Warning! A dentist recently asked me if I thought it would be a good idea to tell his existing patients that he would give them $100 for every new patient they referred. My response was, "Absolutely not!" First of all many state dental boards consider this unethical. Plus, not only will this backfire and not generate referrals, it will send the opposite message that you want. It communicates that this is about money to you, not about care. People will refer to you because they think you're a great dentist, not because they are on commission. It again comes down to human nature. Studies show people are much more willing to refer something good if the only incentive is that their friend or relative will benefit. There's a tremendous difference between an incentive (dangling a carrot) and a token of gratitude after the fact.

LOYALTY TIP #2: PUT PERSONAL INFORMATION INTO YOUR SOFTWARE.

Use your intake forms to gather useful personal information about your patients—such as their hobbies, favorite music, kids' or grandkids' names—and update it periodically, along with their health history form. Then each day as you look at who is coming into the office, review some of these notes with your staff. When you mention these details to a patient in your chair, not only will they think you have the best memory in the universe, they'll also feel that you really care about them as an individual (otherwise known as Goal #1). Nowadays, virtually all practice software can insert a photo of a patient. Have a simple computer camera that can take a snapshot of the patient, so when they come into the office you can recognize them immediately and greet them by name.

LOYALTY TIP #3: DO FREE ANNIVERSARY WHITENINGS.

If you've kept your software up to date with personal information, you will know when a special anniversary may be coming up for a patient. If it's a milestone anniversary, offer to do a complimentary whitening for them. Send them a note or give them a call and say, "Look, we understand your anniversary is coming up. You're probably going to be taking some pictures, and we'd like to offer you both complimentary teeth whitening because you've been great patients of ours." They may or may not do it, but they'll never forget that you said that. And if they do whiten their teeth, think of the conversations it may start:

> "My goodness, look at these pictures. You look fantastic! You look just like you did when you got married."

> "Oh, yes, our dentist whitened our teeth as our anniversary gift."

"Your dentist did what? My dentist doesn't do that. He doesn't even know who I am. He's never offered me anything for free. He double-charges me, I think."

Sounds like the unexpected, doesn't it? It costs you a $75 whitening kit, and if you schedule it during an open time in an assistant's schedule, that's all you're out of pocket.

LOYALTY TIP #4: GIVE YOUR PATIENT A "COMFORT BREAK."

Successful practices make it a priority to let patients know that they care. This often can take as little as a minute of your time, or your staff's time, stopping to ask about their kids, to tell a joke or share a story. My dentist was doing a rather long and unpleasant crown restoration on me a few years ago, and right in the middle he stopped and said, "Why don't we let your mouth calm down a little bit? We've done a lot so far, and we're more than halfway finished. So...have you been to a Lakers® game lately?" We talked for about two minutes, and then he continued with treatment—but in that two minutes, he let me know that he cared about my comfort, and he appreciated who I was as a person. (He somehow remembered I was a Lakers fan. I suspect it's in my patient file somewhere, knowing this guy.)

By giving me a "comfort break," my dentist told me that he understood that dentistry, especially for me on that day, wasn't fun. It took two minutes and it changed the whole experience. Compassion goes a long way. He also did something else I appreciated. He told me I was more than halfway done with the procedure. Most of the time we as patients have no idea how long the procedure is actually going to take. While we're sitting there, it seems like it's going to go on forever. What he did played into basic human psychology, a phenomenon which I can't even explain but we all know is true: When we reach the halfway point, things start to get easier. We can see the light at the end of the tunnel and it relieves our anxiety. I'm sure you have this experience when you're exercising. The first five or ten minutes are pure drudgery, but as you hit that halfway mark it starts to feel like it's all downhill. It's the same way with anything unpleasant. Rounding the bend seems to make it much more tolerable. So give your patients a comfort break, and be sure to tell them that they've passed the halfway point.

Another dentist I know will stop in the middle of a long procedure and have his assistant press on the acupressure points in the patient's jaw. This releases the tension in the jaw and makes the second half of the procedure go more easily for both patient and the dentist. Brilliant. Cost? Two minutes of chairside time. Value? Priceless. Most dentists wouldn't ever think of it (and wouldn't do it even if they did), but as a patient, I can tell you an hour is a heck of a long time to hold your mouth wide open. This is subtle stuff, but it makes a huge difference.

LOYALTY TIP #5: SEND BIRTHDAY FLOWERS (TO GUYS TOO!).

You've heard this before, I'm sure. But once you get past 35, people start forgetting your birthday in a big way. Many times those flowers that you send—to their office of course—might be the only acknowledgment of the occasion. I say send them to guys too, because women notice flowers, especially if they're on a man's desk. What a great way to say, "You're like family to us. Happy birthday!" People will talk—and your patient will remember. Do this for big birthdays (35, 40, 50) and make sure you email or text them on the rest of their birthdays.

LOYALTY TIP #6: APPLY LIP BALM DURING LONG PROCEDURES.

If you're going to try to stretch somebody's mouth to twice the normal size, put a little lip balm on beforehand. It eliminates one of the negative reminders of the dental visit—the cracked, dry lips. It doesn't take a lot of time (and it doesn't take a lot of lip balm), but it goes a long way toward saying you get it.

LOYALTY TIP #7: OFFER COURTESY RIDES ON BIG CASES.

If you have a big case, tell the patient, "Look, we know you're coming in on Tuesday. You're going to be here for quite a while, you're going to be under anesthesia and you might be a little woozy when you go home. We'd like to have a driver pick you up and then take you home. Will that be all right?"

Now, you can probably make a deal with a local limo company or car service for less than $100 round trip. If you have a $5-10,000 case, and you can't build that into the cost of the procedure, then your pricing is all wrong. And here's the reality: Maybe 1 out of 10 people—or 1 out of 20—will actually accept, but *every single one of them will remember that you offered*. You will give them an unexpected experience without actually doing anything, but the fact that you thought about their comfort says, "We care about you."

Now, at one point, as a promotion for 1-800-DENTIST, we sent out postcards with loyalty tips to potential members. One dentist sent the one about the courtesy ride back to me, and had handwritten on it, "Are you out of your f***ing mind?" (See Figure 5. I edited his expletive.)

Figure 5

This doctor ripped his name off the address label so I wouldn't know who he was, but he actually took the time to write this and mail it back to me. You know why? Because he has plenty of spare time. Not only does he think this isn't something he would do—he thinks it's *insane*. "Take care of people? Offer something that considers their condition? Are you out of your mind?"

Maybe I am. Maybe the really successful dentists all around the country are all out of their minds. (I think they're out of their minds with happiness from enjoying their day and having patients who appreciate what they do.) But this is the beautiful thing about this story: The people who think this quality of service is insane are your dental competition!!! Could they make it any easier for you to do something memorable and unexpected?!

LOYALTY TIP #8: USE COMFORT-CONSCIOUS TECHNOLOGY.

Lasers. CEREC. IV sedation. Digital radiography. These not only offer you the chance to do procedures differently, they also give the patient a unique and memorable experience. I'll go into technology a bit more in the next chapter, but a quick thought about The Wand™. Some dentists don't like to use it because it slows them down a bit. They'll say, "I give a great shot. I don't know what the problem is." Hey, I give a pretty good punch, but nobody's asking for one. It's still a *shot*. If you can reduce the intensity of the experience by even 20 percent, I say it's worth it.

LOYALTY TIP #9: GIVE AWAY FREE STUFF.

You've been to dental conventions. You've watched your own staff line up for an hour at the Colgate® booth to get $3 of free stuff, and walk around the trade show floor filling their bags like it's Halloween. It's human nature.

It doesn't have to be much. Try to think of something helpful, like a gift pack with a travel toothbrush, floss and something specific to the treatment they received. How about some aftercare instructions, written down clearly so that they might actually follow them? Or, if they've had whitening, give them some fluoride treatment so the sensitivity will decrease and the dehydration will go away faster. For larger cases, throw in a complimentary whitening. If they're getting veneers, throw in the electric toothbrush of your choice. Or you could offer a free whitening for their mate. It just might get their close friends and family to start thinking about their teeth from a cosmetic standpoint too.

If your patient has a case that requires a pain reliever, have individual packets for them to take home that remind them that you care about them and that you understand what they went through.

Whenever possible, free giveaways should identify you somehow. They should have your name, your logo, your phone number, your website—some way of identifying you. And rather than give them a toothbrush for home, why not something they can take traveling, keep in their briefcase or have in the office? A little reminder of you, their wonderful dentist.

LOYALTY TIP #10: HAVE APOLOGY GIFTS ON HAND.

We all make mistakes. We run late, we forget to remind some-one of something, we bill them incorrectly or we don't get their insurance right. The simple solution is to have a stack of apol-ogy gifts on hand to deal with the situation right away. In every supermarket now you'll see a display with 40 different types of gift cards. Buy a variety of them, from Starbucks to Red Lobster, and use them whenever you need to apologize to a patient. Keep a stack of them at the front desk, and let them pick the one they want (and make a note in their patient profile when you do it). If they're not in the office at the time, mail it to them with a brief note. It goes a long way when you acknowledge that you weren't perfect, or that you realize their time is valuable too. These can also be used to thank someone for referring a patient to the office.

LOYALTY TIP #11: HAVE THE DENTIST CALL NEW PATIENTS PERSONALLY.

This isn't just a magic bullet, this is a *platinum* bullet, and it was suggested to me by a master of practice management, Linda Miles. One of the biggest challenges in a practice is no-shows, patients who call because of your advertising, make an appoint-ment and never show up. They put a nice big hole in your sched-ule, which is expensive, annoying and demoralizing. Bizarrely, I often hear dentists blame the front desk for this. I know you need to express your frustration, but how can it be entirely *their* fault? You need to establish a relationship with the patient so that they feel committed to the appointment. Your team can only do so much. You need to carry the ball over the finish line.

Here's what you do: At the end of every day, the front desk should hand you a list of all the new patients who called to schedule their first appointment, whether they came through advertising or word of mouth. Then you, the dentist, should call every single patient and welcome them to the practice. Half of the time, you will get voicemail, but that doesn't matter. Say something like, "Hi, this is Doctor Williams, and I just wanted to personally welcome you to our practice. When you're a patient of ours, you're like family, so if you have any questions for me ahead of time I'd be happy to answer them." If you get them on the phone, answer their questions. But I believe that just leaving the message will be 90 percent effective.

I've seen dentists *eliminate* no-shows with this technique. Why? *No one in health care has ever done this for them!* How can they not be impressed? How can they not feel a connection to the practice?

I've shared this idea with some dentists who have said, "I don't think that will work." I'm sorry, that's just a lame excuse for being unwilling to do anything yourself to build your practice. And you have to love dentists like this because there they are— your peers—making it easy for you again. I have *never* heard of a practice trying this and abandoning it because it didn't work. Try it for a week. How long can this take every day? Five minutes? 10? That's 10 minutes that prevents a one-hour hole in your day. My dog can do the math on that one.

Most dentists go kicking and screaming into this method of eliminating no-shows. They think it's a waste of time, or they don't think the patient really cares, or they think it's the staff's job to get patients in, not theirs. This ignores the potency and effectiveness of this type of phone call. My suggestion to office managers who have dentists who feel this way is to ask them to just do it for a single week. After that, if they don't think it's worth it, don't bring it up again. What will likely happen, and I've seen it over and over and over again, is that the dentist will find that she actually enjoys the process.

I've even had some dentists tell me that it's the best part of their day. It washes away all of the stress and annoyance of the work-day as they welcome new patients to their practice. They also tell me that they find out very interesting things ahead of time that they would not have known about the patient. Maybe that patient is fearful or had a negative experience once before. This is good to know in advance. Maybe the patient is about to get married and is thinking about veneers. Another patient may have financial or other life issues like a divorce or job loss that makes the idea of restoring their teeth either less or more inter-esting. This informs the direction of the initial case presentation. So it's a marketing tool–One that begins the relationship in a very powerful way. And it just doesn't take that much time.

This falls into the basic philosophy of change: If you want dif-ferent results, do something different. Try it for a week.

You can even take this one step further. When a new patient calls as a result of your advertising, your front desk should make the appointment, but before they hang up, ask if the pa-tient would like to talk to the dentist. Most people will say that it's not necessary, but they will be pleasantly surprised that you asked. Don't worry, they won't assume that your practice is so slow that you have time to talk to anyone. Why not? Because your appointment coordinator is going to say, "The doctor's very busy right now, but I'm sure he could take a minute or two to answer any questions you might have before you come in. Would you like to speak with him?"

In either situation, when the dentist is talking to the patient directly, even for two minutes, the whole context has changed. It is no longer about money or insurance or inconvenience. It's about personalized care. And it's marketing magic.

In the next chapter we'll talk about how you can infuse that kind of magic into every aspect of your office environment.

ACTION ITEMS:

1. Allocate part of your marketing budget for gifts and apology cards. Make sure to reward patients who refer you good cases. Send them a bottle of wine, a bottle of champagne, flowers or something else that expresses your appreciation like a gift card, and use gift cards to smooth over mistakes. Do handwritten thank you notes.

2. Look at your schedule each day and ask yourself who's loyal, have they referred to us (another easy report to run if you're entering the data properly) and what can we do that would be unexpected for them?

3. Incorporate comfort breaks and new patient welcome calls from the dentist as standard operating procedure.

CHAPTER 13

TRANSFORMING YOUR OFFICE INTO A MARKETING ENVIRONMENT

The next time you go to Las Vegas I want you to pay particular attention to something. If you walk into one of the older hotels, like some of the lower-end casinos on Fremont Street, you'll notice they smell like cigarette smoke, alcohol and the sweat of people losing their latest paycheck. However, if you go into Bellagio® or The Venetian®, the second you walk in the air smells wonderful. Why? Because they are pumping a custom-designed scent through the entire ventilation system. You can bet they spent thousands developing it, and thousands more to keep it in the air.

Think environment doesn't matter in business? It matters plenty. Everything is marketing, and your office environment is one of the most neglected and most critical aspects of your marketing. What people see, hear and smell has a profound effect, and although it's often very subtle, it makes huge differences in case acceptance and patient loyalty.

Do you consider the sounds and smells of your office? What can patients hear when they're sitting in the waiting room? What can they hear when they're in the next operatory? Can they hear you talking to another patient—or talking *about* a patient? They should never hear those things. They shouldn't hear drills and, HIPAA requirements aside, they don't need to hear about another person's dentistry. Is your lighting harsh or comforting? Is there music? What are staff members saying? What are they wearing? These are critical questions, because you are in a retail service profession.

Here's my rule of thumb: Think about what a typical old-style physician's office would be like, and do the opposite. It's the perfect paradigm for terrible marketing. Let's go step by step through your office environment. Once you decide to change your environment—to make it a transformational experience from the second patients walk in the door—then a lot of this stuff is easy.

RECEPTION EXPERIENCE

I ask again, do you look like an out-of-date physician's office? You know what I mean. Is the receptionist barricaded behind sliding glass? Have you found some particularly inexpensive chairs for people to sit in, some nice industrial carpeting and off-white paint for the walls? Time to get out the sledgehammer. If anything in your office looks like that, change it.

Your front desk needs to be designed so that staff can get up and greet new patients—face to face, on their feet, shaking their hands and welcoming them to the practice. Your reception should be a welcoming place for new patients, not a barricade that they must fight through for attention. Isn't that what you would want for yourself? Just make it a rule. It's unique. It's unexpected. And it works like magic every time.

Greet people properly. A friend of mine recently went to his dentist and the front desk person asked, "Are you a patient here?" He thought, "No, no, I just like to walk into dental offices randomly. Of course I'm a patient here!" You know what the schedule is. You know who's coming in next. It's Mr. Johnson, most likely. He'll tell you if he's not. He's not going to let you do that root canal if he's not Mr. Johnson. But take a shot.

"Hi, Mr. Johnson. It's so great to see you. Let me give you a tour of the office. Let me tell you about all the training the doctor has. Let me show you our technology. We think you're really going to love our practice. We're so excited to have you here today."

Let's talk about the reception area itself. Have nice furniture—comfortable and clean and fairly new. Have nice colors on the wall and non-industrial surfaces on the floor (no acid-washed concrete). What is the lighting like? If you have harsh fluorescents everywhere, warm it up with incandescent lamps. And provide magazines from this century. Many dentists just stick their old personal magazines in the reception area and think that's enough. Wrong. Not everyone likes golf.

Another thing most dentists pay little or no attention to is the appearance of their forms. Again, you're trying to reinforce that this is not a medical environment. If your patient intake form is a Xerox® of a Xerox of a Xerox, if it's skewed and off-center and kind of fuzzy in the typeface, you know what you communicate? Clinic.

What's worse, do you appreciate what else you're communicating when you look like a medical facility? It's this: Insurance is going to pay for everything—because that's the mindset people have with MDs. That is not the message you're going for.

To me, the ideal scenario is digital intake laptops in reception, because the forms can automatically populate some of the information. That in itself is unique, because it eliminates the need for patients to fill in information that you already know, as if they're a complete stranger. But if you aren't paperless yet, the next best thing is to have nice, colorful forms with your logo on them.

I also highly recommend having PDF (digital) versions of your intake forms available on your website so that new patients can fill them out ahead of time. You could also email them to the new patients. This is convenient for people—hey, even my vet does it now! If the person who takes care of my dog is this advanced, my dentist definitely should be.

Also, as I've mentioned, have specific questions beyond their medical history, like hobbies, anniversaries, grandchildren, etc. And of course, have them rate their own smile and ask what they would change about it if they could.

Should a new patient get a tour? Always! Show them the technology, show them all the diplomas and CE certificates, show them how friendly everyone is. As my friend Imtiaz Manji puts it, you need a "Wall of Fame" in your office that includes all your degrees and CE, before-and-after pictures of patients, letters from them—anything that speaks to your greatness so that your team can brag about the practice in general and the dentist in particular.

SMELL

You probably can't tell what your office smells like because you go there every day, but your patients definitely do notice. In fact, a dentist I know was once turned down for a lease because the landlord said, "I don't want the smell of a dental practice in the building." This guy had a very clear sense of what a dentist's office smelled like, and it was not positive. The most powerful memory trigger is smell, and it's the easiest thing in the world to fix. Aromatherapy costs around $30 a year, and can make your reception and operatories smell like lemongrass instead of burning bone.

MUSIC AND VIDEO

Do patients have options as to what they can hear and watch? These days you can get iPods® loaded with TV shows that patients can watch with special AV glasses. Are there TVs in the operatories? Then give them the remote.

What does your on-hold music or message sound like? Have them be pleasant and informative about your practice benefits.

YOUR SCRUBS

People hate hospitals. Why dress like you're in one? There are hundreds of stylish and flattering variations of scrubs out there, many that you could put your logo on. Which leads me to...

YOUR LOGO

Have one. Get it designed by a graphic designer who specifically does logos. You're trying to create a brand for yourself. A logo is step one.

YOUR PRACTICE NAME

Fifty percent of dental practices are eponymous, that is, they have the same name as the dentist. Probably another 15-20 percent are called "Family Dental." That's fairly generic, plus the concept of a *family dental office* actually repels a certain number of people. They picture a waiting room full of kids running around, and it's those same 45- to 75-year-olds who need significant restorative work.

The essence of branding is to create a unique name directly associated with your business. You might be able to achieve this using your own name, but then what if you add an associate?

The more patients equate you with the brand, the less they will want to see the other doctors. Even worse, when you try to sell the practice, the more patients associate the dentistry in the practice with you and your name, the less value there will be to the new buyer. That seems fairly critical to me, since one of your biggest assets is your practice.

Let me put it another way. What costs more, a generic product or a brand name? That makes it easy, doesn't it? Even if you're in a strip mall, and the best thing you can put out on the sign is "DENTIST" (because the sign has eight different business names on it), be branded in and on your actual practice.

Have a distinct, pleasant, memorable name. Don't be cute and don't be obscure. Be clear and memorable. One way is to use the name of your town, village or area, and spice it up a little. "Brentwood Smiles," for example. Or "Jackson Modern Dentistry Center." And this is very important: Make sure the domain name is available. (I'm talking about ".com," not ".net" or dot-anything else.) It makes a significant difference in search optimization.

Companies spend hundreds of thousands of dollars coming up with brand names for their products and services. It behooves you to spend some time creating a name for yourself, literally.

YOUR TECHNOLOGY

This is a big one, so I'm going to spend some time on it. Technology sells dentistry. It's that simple. We live in a fast-paced, every-year-a-new-cell-phone society. But in the average person's mind, dentistry hasn't changed much in 30 years. (Unfortunately, in some practices it hasn't.) When a patient walks into a dental practice and realizes that there's an entire array of new technology capable of making their experience more comfortable and efficient, with longer-lasting results, then their opinion of dentistry changes. And that's a good thing.

As I've said before, much of the public isn't very aware of all the great benefits that dentistry provides them. But technology will impress them. The problem is, dentists often approach adding new technology like an engineer—purchasing equipment that suits their needs, makes them faster or makes their work easier. But the most important dual role that dental technology plays, in my mind, is to increase case acceptance and word of mouth.

Embedded in this role is a very important and somewhat counterintuitive principle: *Technology pays for itself as a marketing tool even better than it does as a time- or money-saver.*

I'll explain this in greater detail in a moment, but before we get to that, let's look at a direct feedback quote we received from a 1-800-DENTIST caller. She said:

"I appreciated being given a tour of the office and seeing and hearing about all the latest equipment. It really made me feel more at ease. The staff was extremely caring and the treatment was so comfortable that I nearly fell asleep while getting my teeth cleaned! Thanks for the fantastic referral to our new family dentist."

Note something significant that she tells us: *She was put at ease by the technology.* The treatment was so comfortable that she practically fell asleep—that's the sort of thing you want to promote. Making your patients more comfortable is always a worthwhile investment and if you don't do it, you are going to suffer when it comes to your case acceptance. People buy when they are comfortable, when they are trusting and when they think you care.

This story also reveals a subliminal effect. The fact is that none of the fancy technology was even used on her! She was put at ease by its existence, by the fact that the dentist had it and showed it to her as a part of her office tour. Are you not the same in this regard? When you walk into a hospital, don't you want it to be the best-equipped hospital in the country? I sure do. Even though you don't want them to *use* any of that equipment on you, ideally you want to know they have it and that it's the latest and greatest available. Why not provide that same level of comfort and reassurance for your patients?

The reason for this effect is that technology also sends an emotional message—you have this equipment because you care about your patients. You know how important I believe this is from previous chapters. Be the practitioner who cares and who demonstrates it by getting training, buying technology and learning to use it.

Take digital radiography as an example. Some dentists will argue that they prefer the resolution of traditional X-rays. But with digital X-rays, you can show the patient everything that is going on with their teeth, blown up to full-screen size. This creates a powerful impression. A patient can't see a lesion on a tiny X-ray on a wall-mounted light box. (And if they can, it won't appear significant to their untrained eye.) However, you show someone a giant image of decay about to reach the root of their tooth, and they're going to be leaping at you to start their treatment.

What's more, this is only one aspect of digital imaging. You can also store the image more easily, send it out for consultation more efficiently, have it readily accessible to send to insurance companies and on top of all of this, digital X-rays significantly reduce the amount of radiation your patients are exposed to. But none of this matters if you don't tell the patient!

> **"Technology fails as a marketing tool if the patient doesn't know about it."**

Technology fails as a marketing tool if the patient doesn't know about it. And it fails if you just tell them what it does, not how it makes their life better. Make sure they know the benefits to them. Remember, they may not need the equipment for *their* treatment, but you don't know who they know that might—or who might be impressed when your patient starts bragging about your high-tech office (which is why I harp on the idea of a tour for every new patient).

If you have CEREC or other CAD/CAM technology, it should be the highlight of your tour. You or your team member should say something along these lines: "We have this amazing new technology that allows us to do crowns in a single visit. Very few practices have this, but we appreciate how important your time is, so that's why we have it. Even better, we can now do any type of filling with real porcelain, which lasts much longer and matches your teeth perfectly."

Notice I didn't suggest going into what version of the software you have or how much it saves you on your lab bill. That's not marketing. Tell people about the benefits to *them*—clearly and repeatedly.

A dentist recently asked me how she could stand out among all the competition in her immediate area. I asked her if anyone else had a CEREC. She said no. "Simple," I said. "Get one, and make sure every one of your patients knows about the advantage that you are providing them—and then advertise it." The latest technology makes you unique.

Now, some dentists might say, "Yes, but I'd have to do 15 crowns a month with a CEREC in order to justify the cost." Okay, on a basic calculation maybe that's true. But that still only amounts to a crown every other day. But what if you give your patients the option to have porcelain instead of composite whenever you do a filling or an inlay? Make sure they understand that it will match their teeth better and last substantially longer, and it only costs another $100 for the treatment. Many, many people will say yes. People don't want to have to experience restorations more than once, even if it costs a little extra to avoid it. Combine these little upgrades with the crowns you'll be doing and all of a sudden the CEREC is *making* you money.

But equally important is that it's making a powerful impression. This dentist can now say that she's the only dentist in the area with this technology. And believe me, when people hear about CEREC, they are amazed at what it does. A 3-D camera, a computerized lathe, a new crown in six minutes—this is *Star Wars*® stuff!

Another example I mentioned earlier is The Wand. Some dentists complain that The Wand takes longer to complete an injection. *But in exchange, it makes the patient more comfortable.* What's really the priority here—gaining a few seconds per injection, or giving your patients a better experience? There are three things that patients hate most in the dentist office: drilling, shots and having an impression taken. Today, the technology exists to replace them with more comfortable alternatives. Why not reduce the impact of at least one of them?

And what about the third one, impressions? This is the new frontier. For many people, taking impressions may not be a big deal, but start asking your patients about it and you're bound to discover many of them who can't stand the process. Many people have sensitive gag reflexes and while it may not be as traumatizing as a bad experience with a drill, it's not pleasant. With the introduction of digital impression technology, you have a great new opportunity to make the experience your patients have in your practice more comfortable, and even better, to do it before most of your peers. Keep an eye on it.

Finally, while it's on the expensive end of the equipment spectrum, 3-D cone beam technology such as Sirona's GALILEOS™ can make an enormous difference in a practice. I really believe that if you're doing implants, you are at risk of losing a lawsuit should anything go wrong with an implant if you do not have three-dimensional imagery to back up your treatment. But from a marketing standpoint, nothing comes close to impressing your patients more than being able to show them a 3-D display of all the soft and hard tissue in their head. It blows people away.

This technology will also allow you to treat sleep apnea better, do a much wider range of implant cases if you are a GP, and also be better prepared with ortho cases. Sounds like a few ways to make money there. I know practices with a scanner that scan every single patient, regardless of the condition of their teeth, just to be able to show off the technology. You never know. You might just find something important and save their life. But even if you don't, you'll impress them—and they'll tell people about it.

And isn't that what you want, after all? You want to be known as the best-equipped dentist in the area. My advice is, along with using the other devices I've talked about, have a soft-tissue laser, do cancer screenings, do ultrasonic prophys and stay current on all the latest technologies. There's a cost associated with all of this, of course, and you need to pace your purchases—but always weigh the marketing benefit to your practice, not just the expense of the purchase or lease.

In short, adding technology is boosting your marketing power. As the Bonnie Raitt song goes, "Let's give them something to talk about!"

HOW YOU COLLECT MONEY

As I said in Chapter 2, one of the ways that you communicate the value of your service is how you collect money. Step one, of course, is believing that dentistry is a great investment. The next step is collecting money as if you believe that.

Let me repeat my example of high-end restaurants, where they will ask for a credit card when you make your reservation—if you don't show, they will charge you anyway. That's because they only have one chance to use that table at that time, and if they don't make money on it, they lose the chance. Just like you. If you give people terms, if you never charge for missed appointments, if you have massive receivables, you are very effectively communicating that your time is not valuable, and people will treat it that way. When people respect your time, they respect your appointment schedule. You communicate that value by informing them, as nicely as possible, that payment needs to be worked out before their treatment starts.

Remember Greg Sawyer, the dentist who charges 100 percent of his fee before starting an implant case? This hasn't slowed his practice down. It's done the opposite. And he's communicated two very important things to the patient. Right out of the gate he's telling the patient that his time is valuable and that he needs to be fully paid for his services. But beyond that, what the patient infers from this is that Dr. Sawyer is actually the best dentist to do the case *because of the way he charges*. We just naturally assume that when someone charges the most, and insists on getting paid, they must be the best. That's a pretty sweet marketing message.

And don't forget my advice about emergencies. Make them aware that they need to be able to pay at the time of the emergency office visit. Get the relationship started right, with them valuing your time, especially after hours.

YOUR HOURS

Remember, you are in a retail service business, so have hours that accommodate your patients. Open early once a week and stay late once a week. Most of the time this works fine for your team, and some even appreciate the flexibility it gives them. Open every Saturday and skip Wednesday or Thursday. At least be open every *other* Saturday. You'll find that these extra hours will fill up first, and that should tell you something about what your patients want.

My friend Dr. Mark Morin, who is a CEREC savant and runs an amazingly successful practice in Detroit, explains it perfectly. He says, "Am I open weekends? You bet I am. You give me a big case, I'll be in there Sunday night if that's the only time the patient can do it." That's service. And that's how to build a practice.

THE LANGUAGES YOUR PRACTICE SPEAKS

Dr. Bill Dorfman, probably the most famous dentist in the country, is a brilliant practice builder. As long as I've known him, which is over 20 years, he has had French-speaking clientele as part of his practice in Los Angeles (he learned French in school in Switzerland). You may ask, how many French people are there in LA? Well, how many patients do you need to build a successful side practice, 1,000? I can assure you that there are plenty more than 1,000 French-speaking people in LA, and I'll bet they all know that their language is spoken at Dr. Dorfman's. He needs to do virtually no advertising to get these patients.

This brings up a very significant point. Even if people know English as their second language, *they generally prefer to speak about health care in their native tongue.* We are an immigrant nation. Knowing a second language, or hiring a staff member who speaks one fluently, gives you something unique, and unique equals a marketing advantage. Spanish is the obvious choice in most cities, but look at the demographics of your town. What is the growing ethnicity? Usually, immigrants build a middle class within a generation. Cater to them, and you will end up treating the whole family—and their neighbors too.

Here's another brilliant suggestion from Linda Miles. One of her clients mentioned to her that Mercedes was building a new plant in his town. She suggested that he print a batch of business cards in German (on one side) and drop them off at the HR department. Guess who got all of the German-speaking patients?

Finding a language niche in your area and catering to them is a phenomenal practice builder, and it creates extremely loyal patients.

YOUR GENDER

Sad to say, guys, but many people would actually prefer a female dentist to a male one. I'm not recommending a sex change operation for the men, but I would be seriously looking for a female associate. If you are a woman, make sure that you are prominently featured in your advertising.

THE DOCTOR'S CLOTHES AND GROOMING

I think the goal for a dentist's attire is to strike a balance between professional and comfortably stylish. You can create your own style, of course (and I recommend that), but it needs to be distinguished as well as distinct. When I see a dentist in scrubs with a long-sleeved t-shirt underneath (and I've seen this plenty), I think hospital orderly, not dental professional. Are Hawaiian shirts your thing? Maybe. Just don't let them be so faded that they are obviously five years old.

Also, I spend a lot of time at dental conventions, and I am always amazed when a dentist comes up to the booth and has a noticeable level of dandruff on his dark blazer. I'm sorry, but dandruff is not some incurable disease. If I'm looking up at my dentist with my mouth wide open and I see a flaking scalp, I'm out of there.

Even more remarkable is when a dentist's own teeth are a mess. Nothing destroys confidence like a dentist who doesn't believe in dentistry. Most likely these dentists are not reading this book, but if you are, find a good dentist now! Call 1-800-DENTIST if you have to.

TEAM MEMBERS' TEETH

Your entire team should all have fabulous teeth, and they should have you to thank for it. They are the best advertisement for your dentistry. Do it in your spare time, but make sure everyone's smile is exemplary.

PUTTING IT ALL TOGETHER

It comes down to this: What is the experience of a patient who comes to your office, from the second you answer the phone or the first view of your website, all the way through to them paying, leaving, going out on the street and talking about the dentistry you did for them?

I have two guiding principles that I use: The first I shared with you, which is do the opposite of what an old-school MD practice would do. The second is, ask yourself what a retail service business *would* do. As you go into retail businesses, start to notice the unique things they do to attract, greet and retain customers. Gradually, you'll start to see ways to change your practice and infuse marketing into every aspect of it. The results will be almost instantly noticeable. It will also be a much more fun place to be for both you and your staff.

This is my last note on office environment: Is your office fun? That will affect how your patients feel when they come to your office. Make the extra effort to be a happy environment. A lot of that boils down to the attitude of your staff, which is the subject of the next chapter.

ACTION ITEMS:

1. Go through your office and see where your environment is falling short. Make a step-by-step plan to fix each thing.

2. Plan your office tour, practice it and make sure everyone knows it.

3. Tech up! Don't look at it as an expense. Plan it out as a marketing approach as well as a clinical approach. And incorporate each new technology into your tour and staff scripts, as well as your website and advertising. Stay ahead of the curve.

CHAPTER 14

TEAM ATTITUDE

I was in Bangkok a few years ago, and one morning I was walking down the main avenue outside my hotel. Now, at night this street is packed with people—Thai citizens shopping, tourists and hundreds of street vendors, all crammed on the sidewalks—so by morning the street is trashed. On this particular day, one of the storm drains had gotten clogged and a group of workers had assembled to clean it out. They lifted a large concrete lid, about four feet long, from the drain to reveal a brown, filthy pool of water. (See Figure 6.)

As I walked by, one of the workers, who was in shorts, kicked off his flip flops and climbed into the dirty water *up to his waist!* He began to use a pole to clean out the clogged drain. (See Figure 7.) What I found most remarkable though, was that this guy was *cheerful!* He was smiling, joking with his coworkers and acting remarkably amiable. I myself would probably have climbed into a river full of piranhas before I climbed into this storm drain. Right then it occurred to me—if this guy can be cheerful, then nobody who works in a dental practice has anything to complain about.

Figure 6

Figure 7

The key to a good team is finding people with the right attitude. I will now tell you an iron-clad rule of business: You cannot make a miserable person happy. You do not have the managerial skills, the psychological training or enough money to turn their misery into happiness, and even if you did, why would you spend your time that way? There are people who are naturally happy, and I've found that a good attitude is a choice a person makes, not a reaction to their life. And a team with a great attitude is the best marketing there is.

At 1-800-DENTIST, we have a 24-hour call center. Operators are chosen based on two criteria: the ability to speak English clearly and the ability to be compassionate and pleasant all day long. I can teach them dental terminology, how to use my software and any other business skills. But I can't make them positive. They have to start that way.

There are people everywhere with difficult lives, painful challenges and deep sorrow, and yet they are pleasant, kind and generally always in good spirits. Then there are people who have had

"A team with a great attitude is the best marketing there is."

the red carpet laid out for them every day of their lives, and yet they are depressed, pessimistic complainers. I'll say it again: A good attitude is a choice, not a reaction. Find people who make that choice, and life will be beautiful—and your practice will thrive.

What do you do with your current staff? The answer is simple. Get rid of the miserable people (and your whole team knows who they are), because this is the corollary to the iron-clad rule that you cannot make miserable people happy: *They will make your happy people miserable.*

Now it's easy for me to say, "Get rid of them," but I know how hard it is. You think that your practice will fall apart; you don't know how you'll replace them; you don't have time to find someone else; you're afraid they'll sue you—I've heard, and probably said, all of those excuses myself. I currently have 250 employees. I've been in business since 1986, and several of my friends own businesses, some of them quite large. Every one of them would agree with me when I say that *I have never regretted firing anyone, only how long I waited to do so.*

There is a great system of evaluating your employees that came from Jack Welch, the former CEO of GE®, who is a master of business management. Basically, you rate your employees as A, B or C players. A-players have a great attitude, do their job well, always strive to get better and take the success of the business personally. B-players do a good job, but are still learning. They are committed to the success of the business, but need some refinement. C-players are clock punchers who cut corners, complain and do the minimum it takes to not get fired.

Take 10 minutes and rate everyone in the practice. I'll bet you can do it in two minutes. You know what I'm going to say next: Make a plan to let all the C-players go.

The day you do, everyone else in the office will respect you again. Why? The fact is, as long as you tolerate C-players, the rest of the team not only loses respect for you, they resent you for making them work with C-players. And something else more insidious is happening: The C-players are turning your A-players into B-players. The A-players are spending their day thinking, "Why am I busting my butt and doing my job plus half of hers? I'm just going to do what's necessary."

I know it feels harsh to let someone go, especially if they've been with you a while. But in the end, I believe that you are doing them a favor. You're giving them an important life lesson that they can't bring negativity, inefficiency or anything but their best to the workplace. Hopefully they will absorb that lesson, but that's not really your responsibility.

There is a reason severance pay was created. Business owners figured out that it would be worth the money to actually pay people to stop working for them. It sounds nutty, but it's been proven countless times.

Here's an added bonus to taking strong action: When the C-players are gone, then the B-players start striving to be A-players. Doesn't that sound nice?

HOW DO YOU FIND GOOD TEAM MEMBERS?

I hear dentists complain all the time that they can't find good team members—except for a few who have figured it out. A dental practice is a peculiar business environment in that there is almost no opportunity for promotion. In most businesses, the opportunity to move up is one of the attractions of a job.

In a dental practice, you only have two ways to attract and keep good employees: love or money. And I recommend both.

They will feel loved, and they will in turn love their job, because you have made the office a fun place to show up to and have eliminated the miserable people and the C-players. Now you need to deal with money.

The dentists I know who have no trouble attracting employees solve the money problem this way: They pay more to get the better people. Genius, isn't it? The economic reality is that when your practice is fully productive, and you grow past that threshold where you have met your overhead, your profit margin can be 40 percent or more. So share it. Pay your staff 5-10 percent higher than market average, and incentivize them based on the success of the practice. To pay your entire staff 10 percent more than you do now would take approximately 3 percent of your profit away, but in time would probably increase your gross by 30 percent. Plus you could probably increase your fees 3 percent and your patients would hardly notice.

> "You have only two ways to attract good employees: love or money."

You don't necessarily have to increase your current employees' pay, but if you don't have an incentive plan, you are missing the biggest boost to your growth. Here's how a dentist friend (and longtime client) of mine, Dr. Parimal Kansagra, approaches pay with new employees. He first asks them what they expect to make as a salary. Then he says, "I'm going to pay you

5 percent more than that number, and here is what I expect from you in return." Then he spells out not only the job duties, but their need to have a positive attitude and work well with the entire team. Finally, he ices the cake by telling them about his incentive plan.

What happens is everyone starts doing whatever it takes to grow the practice. And if someone isn't, you won't have to address it with them—the other team members will do it for you.

One more word about incentive plans: Bonus the staff as a team. Individual bonuses on production tend to obliterate the team effort. You can bonus in a ratio based on a percentage of their salary. My pal Imtiaz Manji recommends that you put half their bonus into the employee's personal retirement fund—either 401(k) or IRA—and I love the idea. This way you're helping them save for their future with what is essentially extra money. Once that amount starts to grow, your staff loyalty will grow in direct proportion.

There is one situation where a small individualized incentive program works wonders. It's designed to get team members to grab that phone and focus on getting the patients in the door. It's very simple. Give a $10 bonus to anyone who gets a new patient in. Dr. Ron Groba and his wife Marie are long-time 1-800-DENTIST members who advise other dentists on how to be successful. Marie tells me that once she instituted this incentive, team members were literally diving for the phone, when they used to let it ring and ring. It's worth every penny of the $10. (In fact, I think it's probably worth $50, but I don't want to tell Marie's team that!)

"Wait a minute," you say. "Why is Fred giving hiring and management advice?" As I said at the beginning of the chapter, a good team is good marketing—maybe the best marketing you can do.

I recently became friends with Tony Hsieh, the CEO of Zappos®, the billion-dollar-a-year online clothing company. His company has a unique policy where, after two weeks of mandatory training, each employee is offered $2,000 to quit. The reasoning is that if the person doesn't want to work there, and is just staying until they find another job, they would rather the person move on now and not hang around. But if the person refuses the money and stays, then that new employee is making a powerful, positive statement that Zappos is where he wants to work. It's brilliant.

Further insight into the importance of staff attitude is revealed by a story I heard at a seminar presented by The Ritz-Carlton® hotel chain. If you recall, one of my recommendations throughout the book has been to study retail service businesses, and the hospitality industry often provides great inspiration. Ritz-Carlton prides itself on a high level of service, and they have codified 29 rules of service that every single employee has to know and follow.

In an effort to refine their service, the hotel did a survey of guests in which they attempted to determine the reasons why customers had stopped staying at Ritz-Carlton hotels. They found one dominant response. A whopping 67 percent of respondents said it was because of the indifference of a single Ritz-Carlton employee. Not the rudeness, not the meanness, not the poor service—the *indifference!* Of a *single employee! And they never came back.* Think of how subtle that is.

Think about how much indifference people are used to in health care. Don't be guilty of the same offense, because they can easily find another dentist. People respond to being treated nicely.

An important question you need to ask yourself (if you are the dentist) is, "Who am I in my practice?" That is, what is your personality type? Are you gregarious? Are you naturally outgoing, talkative, friendly, can't wait to meet people? Are you naturally empathetic? Are you low-key or energetic? Are you good at talking to people and persuading them to do something right away or do you need to build a relationship first? Are you organized? If you don't know the answers to these questions, ask your team. If they won't tell you, ask your spouse. He or she will generally clear it up for you with some very concise observations, and won't be as gentle as your team!

You need to know this about yourself, because *you don't have to be any of these things!* You just have to be a great practitioner. Fill in the gaps with team members who have the skills and qualities you might be missing. You have an environment with many people, all interacting with your patients. You're not going to undergo a sudden personality change just because I told you to. Assess who you really are—be honest with yourself—and then just hire the support that helps you to create the ideal marketing environment.

If you are the office manager, do this exercise with your dentist or dentists. Have a candid conversation about it, and then shape your team accordingly.

Finally, when it comes to staff attitude, there is no place more important than the front desk. And I have a special recommendation here: Look outside of dentistry for your front desk people. Don't get hung up on whether they understand the business yet or not. Most of the time, if they came from another dental office they have preconceived notions and often negative associations with patients. Seek out people whose personality is absolutely effervescent. You can teach them the software, billing and everything else. Get someone with energy, enthusiasm and an overwhelmingly positive attitude and you're a lot more than halfway there.

In the next chapter, we'll discuss the single largest roadblock to a practice's success: the telephone.

ACTION ITEMS:

1. Acknowledge who the C-players and *Les Miserables* are, and show them the door.

2. Sit down every day with your appointment schedule and your team in your morning huddle and decide whose life you're going to change that day. It's a great way to jumpstart that good attitude.

3. Create a bonus plan for the whole team, and also put in place a $10 incentive for each new patient appointed by any team member.

CHAPTER 15

THE ALMIGHTY
TELEPHONE

The most valuable piece of technology in your practice is not the high-speed drill. It's not your computers or your digital radiography. It's the telephone. The telephone is the aorta of your practice. It is the valve through which every new and existing patient flows. And many practices have 90 percent blockage in that artery. It is by far the most overlooked marketing aspect of most dental practices.

Before I ask about how well you answer the phone, I must first ask, "*Do you answer the phone?*" That may seem like an obtuse question. Of course you answer the phone, right?

Here's why I ask. In our call center at 1-800-DENTIST, we can see in every member dentist's profile whether their office is open. When we have a potential patient on the phone, we personally introduce them to the office if they are indeed open (we put the patient on hold and call the practice on a three-way call). Now remember, we can see clearly the office hours.

We know they're there, and yet *25 percent of the time*, the call goes to voicemail. That's one out of four calls! That's not retail service, that's not even service. And it's not just our members who are guilty of this. Consultants have told me that this is true for most practices.

Even worse, a number of practices have answering systems that won't take a message. I get the strategy—if they can't leave a message, then they won't cancel an appointment. Guess what? If a patient wants to cancel, even if they don't reach you, they're still not coming.

Back to not answering the phone. Most dental practices are only open about 35 hours a week. 1-800-DENTIST is open 24 hours a day for one reason: People call us 24 hours a day. In other words, we no longer live in an office-hours world, and most dentists are missing 25 percent of the calls *during* business hours. Imagine what you miss the rest of the time. Is your practice so abundantly successful that you can absorb this level of waste? That would surprise me.

Being curious about this strange phenomenon, I often inquire of practices why they are not picking up the phone when they are open. Most dentists don't even realize this is happening, but their team members do. They have a variety of explanations, from being too busy to thinking someone else is going to pick up. The most bizarre response was a staff member who said, "We don't answer the phone when we're opening the mail."

I was stunned by this. "Doctor's orders," she explained.

Then I pieced it together. At some point, someone messed up a deposit as they were processing the incoming payments, and the dentist said something like, "Okay, from now on, don't do anything else when you're opening the mail." I'm pretty sure he didn't mean clamp off the lifeline of the practice by not answering the phone, but many team members *don't like to answer the phone,* so they immediately included that into the "don't do" list.

And therein lies the problem: Staff often view answering the phone as an interruption or an annoyance. A dental practice is a classic example of, "We could get a heck of a lot more work done if it weren't for all these darn patients."

Another incident illustrates this well. Once at a dental convention, a woman came up to the 1-800-DENTIST booth and told one of my sales reps, Kevin, that her practice was a member, and that in the past two months, even though they had received more than 25 referrals, they had only managed to get two patients to show up in the office. Kevin explained that if the member is receiving the referrals from us but not getting them into the office, this was usually an indicator that something is going wrong at the front desk.

"*I'm* the front desk," she roared, "and I'm perfect! The problem is you call at the most inopportune moments!" I was speechless. When exactly is an inopportune moment to call the office? "Is the phone in the bathroom?" I asked myself. And how could someone calling from outside possibly know that it was indeed the wrong time to be calling? Unfortunately, I know this woman is not alone in her thinking. In fact, I think she's in the majority—and it costs the average practice hundreds of new patients.

I do sympathize. A dental practice is a small business, where almost everyone is multi-tasking and that's a challenge. But there is a solution. It's a business tool called a *priority hierarchy*.

A priority hierarchy is a system where everyone knows the order of importance of every activity or responsibility in the business. Most businesses, especially small businesses, don't have a clear priority hierarchy. They have priorities, like their "four pillars for success," or their "cornerstones of a well-run business." But these business rules don't tell you what to do when you have two conflicting priorities, and you've been told they're both extremely important. This is exactly what setting up a priority hierarchy does.

I'll give you an example (of course, it's from Disney, the masters of customer relations). At any Disney park, the number-one rule—the top of the priority hierarchy—is guest safety. The safety of every single guest at all times trumps anything else that an employee might be doing. If a cast member, as they call their employees, is carrying two sacks of cash over to the main office and sees a guest at risk, his job is to drop the money and help them. Of course he knows the money's important, but he also knows what's *more* important. In fact, he'll lose his job if he chooses to take care of the money and something happens to the guest. Why? Because Disney knows that people equate their brand with safety—that parents know that they can drop their kids off for an entire day and night and nothing's going to happen. All it takes is something going wrong one time and that reputation is severely damaged, costing thousands, if not millions, to fix.

How does this apply to a dental practice? You usually get one chance on the phone—and it's brief—to get a new patient in the office. It won't happen if you don't answer the phone, and answer it well. So my priority hierarchy for a dental practice would be this:

1. Answer the phone within three rings—nicely;
2. Ask for referrals;
3. Ensure a safe and sterile environment.

You can make your own list, but if your number one is not *my* number one, you do it at your own risk.

Let me drive this point home again: If your staff looks at answering the phone as an interruption, or an annoyance, stop advertising immediately. You are wasting your advertising dollars. If I were a dentist and heard the phone hit the fifth ring without someone answering, I'd be snapping the latex off and grabbing the phone myself. That patient in the chair isn't going anywhere. The potential patient is going away fast.

Picking up the phone is square one. They key is to answer it well, because it's estimated that 50 percent of new patients are lost in the first phone call. In my mind, there is one job at the front desk, and that's to get the new or existing patients into the office (not to screen people out or field their questions, but to get them *in* the office).

This is not a skill people are born with. It takes training, focus, the right attitude and the right person. At 1-800-DENTIST, we do a psychological profile on every operator as part of the hiring process to make sure that they can be pleasant, caring and compassionate all day long. Then they get a week of training before they are allowed to take their first phone call. Someone also sits with them for several days afterward, listening to how they handle every call. How much training has your team had on proper call handling? I'm guessing not very much for this very critical role.

Over the years, we've had several dentists leave the 1-800-DENTIST program because they say that the quality of patients isn't good. Yet, when these dentists leave the service, we often immediately replace them with another dentist in the same area, send the *same* type of patients from the same advertising sources and the new office gets approximately 70-80 percent of the patients in (and usually gets a 5-to-1 return on their advertising investment). How can this be?

"Answering the phone well takes focus, training, the right attitude and the right person."

We've narrowed it down to what happens in that first phone call, and who is handling those calls. It can make or break a practice. It comes down to some simple criteria: being pleasant, being focused on that call and understanding the value of that call. I often say that I would rather have a happy idiot at the front desk than a miserable genius. People who are calling a dental practice, especially for the first time, are extremely delicate. They have a lot of apprehension about seeing a dentist, and they have no idea whether they will feel safe with you, whether they can trust you or if you even care about them. What they hear is critical.

You know from your own experience how easy it is to perceive subtle differences on the phone. How long does it take for you to get turned off when you're calling a customer service line, for example? 5 seconds? 10? Just a hint of attitude and they've lost you. You know in seconds if they are attentive or annoyed. Don't you think dental patients can hear that too? And sometimes, your staff is not subtle about their annoyance or impatience. I'm trying to get you 180 degrees from that point, to where they are focused entirely on doing whatever it takes to bring patients in.

Now please don't try to fix this by just telling your front desk to be nice, or to get every patient in. Get them some training. This is a mission-critical position. Don't wing it. And for God's sake don't think it's going to fix itself with a few pointers from me.

Here's another classic horror story: A large implant company recently did an advertising campaign directly to consumers. They handled the calls themselves and then transferred the patient live to a practice that used their implants. The manager in charge of this project related what was one of hundreds of similar stories, but this one obviously was the most traumatic to overhear. They were calling in a large implant case to an oral surgeon, a good client for many years. His receptionist, when told that the patient was looking for dental implants, stated emphatically, "All we do is pull teeth here!" This was actually the receptionist's comprehension of what the practice did. She blew off a $30,000 implant case, and the dentist never knew it happened. (In this case, the dentist may have been better off letting calls go to voicemail!)

The front desk needs to know everything the practice offers, and the benefits of those services to the patient. They need to express genuine concern for the patient, and then—that's right—get them in.

Don't be irritated if callers have insurance questions. Who doesn't? Who even understands dental insurance? What patient understands that it doesn't even resemble their health insurance coverage? Why are you trying to qualify whether you like the patient, if they have enough money or if they're a big enough case? Get them in! Schedule them for a 20-minute consultation. Figure the rest out after they're in the office.

Your whole team also needs to not be judgmental on the phone. People can sense when they are being judged. Remember in the "Reasons People Leave" section of Chapter 8, where some people will actually change dentists because the staff gives them such a guilt trip about how long it's been since their last visit? People don't need that. What's important is that they are (almost) ready to come in now. Get them in.

I would even assign a team member to be responsible for after-hours calls. Have a cell phone dedicated to that, and have each team member take the phone one night a week. And when your answering service has a real emergency, have them call that cell phone. If it's an existing patient calling, you are giving them a higher level of service. If it's a new one, let the team member evaluate how to prioritize the response. You never know who the next big case might be.

Every phone call that is handled poorly is a lost opportunity. What is this waste costing you? Back in Chapter 11, we calculated the value of a new patient—that's the cost to you. That's the long-term production that is lost, and the new patients who are lost, when a new patient call is not handled properly. That's a big number. When that phone rings, it's like someone is about to deliver $30,000 to the practice. Isn't that worth doing extremely well, paying someone appropriately to do it and getting them the proper training to maximize their success?

The most successful method I know for improving the front desk performance is to record the calls, then let your team listen to them and use them for coaching. Don't use it as a reason to fire them. You will find that they can hear the tone of their voice themselves, and they may have an epiphany about it and start smiling and being attentive on the phone. Or you may have a call where they talk for 15 minutes to a person and never ask them if they want to make an appointment. This happens all the time. Hearing themselves do this is the fastest way to get people to change.

Do it for two weeks, and be sure to tell all the callers you're recording them for quality purposes. It's not expensive—often your phone carrier can do it remotely without any new hardware—and there are also training services that can do this and also coach your team. Check the resources in Appendix II.

In the next chapter I'll get deeper into how to maximize your results on the most valuable kind of new patient, one that most practices neglect.

ACTION ITEMS:

1. Lay out your priority hierarchy. Make sure every team member knows it.

2. Get somebody great as your appointment coordinator, and make sure every call is answered, and answered well.

3. Train your entire team to excel on the phone. Record them.

4. Get good after-hours phone coverage.

CHAPTER 16

THE MOST VALUABLE
NEW PATIENT

The most valuable new patient to a dental practice is what I call a *media-generated referral*. This is a patient who comes to your practice from some form of advertising—direct mail, Google Adwords, 1-800-DENTIST—as opposed to word of mouth. Why is this type of patient the most valuable? For one simple reason: *Everybody they know doesn't know you yet.* If you treat them properly and turn them into a loyal patient, they are going to lead you to an entirely new circle of influence: all their friends, family and coworkers.

These patients are the primary source of your word-of-mouth referrals. And while your existing word-of-mouth patients are certainly valuable as a source of referrals, generally you have already reached some of their circle of influence (because they found you through their brother, or their father or their friend in the office). Someone who came to you from advertising can start a whole new referral tree, so to speak.

This obviously ties in directly with my earlier discussion about the lifetime value of a patient. It is not only a matter of what that new patient will spend; we're also talking about what the five people they refer to the practice will spend. And the more effective you are at generating referrals internally, the more you will eventually need new patients through advertising. That's because you will have already treated your existing patient base's friends and family, so you'll need new blood. That makes media-generated referrals all the more valuable.

I spent the whole last chapter beating the drum about answering the phone, answering it effectively and focusing on getting patients in, and this, of course, is crucial with patients from advertising. But now I'm going to go one level deeper, and talk about the two big mistakes that practices generally make with media-generated referrals.

The first is not getting these patients in right away. By that I mean within 24-48 hours. This excludes the weekend, but barely so. We have dealt with millions of media-generated referrals in my business over the years, and the dentists who succeed at converting the majority of their referrals into patients are the ones who follow this rule religiously—because they know that the opportunity diminishes by half every day thereafter. Dr. Howard Farran, the creator of *Dentaltown*®, has an extremely apt description of these types of patients. He calls them *fragile*, because they generally are procrastinators and avoiders who have suddenly reached a point of taking action—and that urge may quickly go away. Get them in. Fast.

Get them in for two reasons: Not only will you miss out on the new patients that they could be sending you, but also you *paid* for the advertising that got them to call.

Many dentists will make excuses for not getting new patients in right away. They don't have enough room in their schedule, the patient might not show up, it's hard to get back to the patient in time to schedule, the patient's schedule and the practice schedule don't allow them to appoint that fast. Those are just excuses, and all they do is create massive missed opportunities. We've talked a lot about human nature throughout the book, and this is what's at play here. As the actress Carrie Fisher once said, "Instant gratification is too slow." That's the world we now live in. So give them what they want right now. That's good marketing.

And who says you have to get them in for a full hour? Bring them in for a quick, 15-minute initial exam. I don't know a dentist in America who can't slide his schedule around enough to accommodate a new patient exam every day. If it seems like they might need more time, but you don't want a no-show blowing your schedule apart, schedule them right before lunch or before the end of the day. That way, if they don't show, you don't do much damage to your schedule. If they do show, and they need a lot of treatment immediately, skip lunch or stay late.

The idea is to give them an experience of your office, and let them see how much you care. And by the way, if the dentist is calling all the new patients ahead of time, there will be a lot fewer no-shows, of that you can be sure.

Let me put it another way. If you're booked out 30 days and you can't or won't squeeze new patients in any sooner, stop advertising. If your staff looks at the phone as an annoyance/interruption, stop advertising.

The second big mistake that people make with media-generated referrals is prejudging them. By that I mean trying to decide if they are somehow right for your practice, or can afford to pay for your dentistry. I'm going to discuss this from two angles: people's attitude toward dental spending and the concept of patient readiness.

This is the reality: The average American doesn't live on a budget, and even if they do, what they budget for dentistry is $0. So that's where you're starting. When a patient has been neglecting their teeth, whatever amount you suggest it will cost will give them sticker shock.

"The average American has budgeted $0 for dentistry."

But here's another reality for most Americans: If we really want something, we find the money for it. This is where believing and communicating that dentistry is a great investment comes in. You never know what people will find the money for, how they will find it or even how much they have. *Especially over the phone!* Bring them in the office, show them what great dentistry can be like and then help them figure out how to get it.

Prejudging patients is as much of a problem once they're in the office. To give you an analogy, a friend of mine in the San Fernando Valley needed a new roof on his home. It wasn't a lavish home, because despite the fact that my friend is loaded, he lives modestly. He is also not a very fashionable dresser and drives an ancient Volvo®. He called a roofing contractor for an estimate, and I'm guessing the roofer took one look at my friend, his worn-out Levi's® and his old car and thought, "This guy's broke." So all the roofer told him about were the basic shingles that he could put on his house and the price. He didn't tell him about fireproof shingles (and this is an area prone to brush fires). He didn't tell him about ceramic tiles or slate (even though slate lasts 100 years, and ceramic tiles last at least 50, and they're both entirely fireproof) because those were all expensive. The roofer decided what he thought my friend could afford, and was worried about overbidding the job. He didn't even consider my friend's basic safety. My friend could've easily put slate on his roof (and in the end, he did—with another roofer). Now, would you consider this roofing contractor a professional or a dope?

But how many dentists practice *exactly* this way? They decide what the patient can afford and that's what they present rather than explaining the patient's different options, their optimal treatment plan or the benefits of comprehensive care. Don't decide what they can afford. They are looking to you to be the professional. They might be shocked at how much dentistry they need, but they may shock *you* with their ability to get the money.

Here's the catch though. They will do it when *they are ready*. Not when you're ready, which is, of course, right now. You need to consider where the patient is in his desire and understanding regarding his dental care. Almost in contradiction to the tendency to under-present is the urgency many dentists feel (particularly when they have a patient who came from advertising, and thus cost them money), to try to make their money back right away. Hold on a moment, Dr. Dazzle.

Think about the last big case you completed. How long had that person been a patient? Most of the time the answer I get from dentists is, "Two or three years." It's not, "She was a brand new patient." Maybe that happens occasionally (and your pals will love to tell you their magical stories of patients who accepted full-mouth reconstruction in the first visit), but that is not the norm, particularly with media-generated referrals.

In fact, you can scare someone away with how much dentistry they need if you haven't first explored something very basic. This point is very basic marketing, as well. You have to first ask them, "Do you want to take care of what's necessary right now, or do you want to talk about more comprehensive care?" Then wait for the answer. Dr. Paul Homoly taught me this concept of patient readiness, as well as many other marvelous things about case presentation, and they all work like gangbusters.

Most patients will be curious about what comprehensive care entails. You should not tell them what it costs at this point. You're painting a picture of their perfect smile. Why slap a price tag on it and spoil the mood? The truth is they are not going to die if they don't do this treatment immediately. Create a relationship with them, and along with it an appreciation of optimum oral health.

I'll say it one more time: Patients accept when they are ready. All they need to know is that when they are, it will change their life. They may not think it's necessary yet, or they may not have figured out that it is worth the money, or they may not have figured out how to get the money (though hopefully you've given them finance options).

Other things may come into play, too. They may decide to get married. They may get divorced. They may have an event coming up where there will be important photographs. Someone may comment on their teeth. (Little kids are great for describing exactly how your teeth look, and usually the news is not good. That can trigger some serious restorative care.) The patient herself might look at old photographs and suddenly notice her teeth have changed color, or cracked or just don't look good anymore, and it happened so gradually she didn't notice it before. Now she's ready.

MARKETING IN THE "FOREVER RECESSION"

The days when a new patient walks in the door and does a full set of veneers and pays for it all at once with their home equity line of credit are pretty much over. A much larger segment of the American population is now living at poverty level, and many companies are dropping dental insurance as a benefit. This is not likely to change back to the gogo 2000s for a long time, if ever, hence the term "forever recession." You need to adapt to this change to survive and thrive. And you can thrive. I see many practices doing it even in the face of double-digit unemployment in their cities and their cosmetic cases dropping. This is what I've found to be true, not just in dentistry, but in all industries: What is going on in the world, the country, your state and your neighborhood is pretty much out of your control, so you have to make your own economy.

I'm going to say that again: *You have to make your own economy.* What this means, in essence, is you focus all your attention and energy on what is in your control, and don't stress about the rest. Easier said than done, I know, but once you do it (and I've seen hundreds of practices do this), you'll know it's true. My friends in other businesses who succeed in this economy have the same approach. If they can't have any effect on something they don't let it affect them. It's a waste of energy.

This is what I recommend:

Don't stop advertising! The biggest mistake small businesses make is to cut their ad budgets when times are hard. The smart businesses increase it, knowing that their competitors are backing off. You may save temporarily by cutting out your advertising spending, but in the end you'll lose money. While it is normally the fuel for your practice growth, advertising is now the fuel for your income stability. Borrow the money if you have to, but keep the engine running.

Realize that the advertising cost per new patient is going to go up, while their initial spending may go down. As I have said, you are in this for the long term. Build your patient base, build your relationships, and when times get better your patients will start to spend on the comprehensive care that you have presented.

Here is my basic recommendation: *Be more accommodating.* Make your hours more convenient. Weekend, early morning and evening hours make it more convenient for people who may not have as much latitude to take time off from work as they did two years ago. If you want production, you have to make it easier for people to see you.

I also suggest that you shift your focus away from cosmetic dentistry. If you heavily advertise cosmetic, back off. Understand that in tight times you will do a lot more restorative work, and your ad dollars will pay off more than if you chase the big cosmetic cases, which will become fewer and fewer.

Give them financing options. Accept all major credit cards. Set up an account with CareCredit® or one of the other outside patient financing companies. But whatever you do, don't finance your work yourself. That's not financing, that's a receivables nightmare. Instead, stretch out the treatment plan to fit their budget and ability to pay. What you may have once done in two big appointments you should now perhaps spread over as much as a year.

Consider taking insurance plans. I know the ideal is to take no insurance, but when people are having trouble figuring out how to pay, you need to still reach your contribution margin threshold, so you need to make it more attractive to a larger group of people. You certainly don't have to accept every HMO, but being at least a PPO provider on some of the more popular plans in your area can keep you busier in tough times.

Sharpen your team's phone skills. Now is when you need to get every single patient in the door. Get professional training from someone like Linda Miles, Katherine Eitel or Jay Geier and you'll see the results immediately. Use digital communications like those offered by PatientActivator to tighten your recall. The more efficiently you remind your patients, the less they will put off their care. And the more you make your entire patient base aware of all your services by communicating with them on a regular basis through digital newsletters and email marketing campaigns, which don't cost you anything, the more you will produce from your existing patients, and the more they will refer to you.

If you're the dentist, sharpen your own skills. The right CE will go a long way. Learn to do implants, improve your speed and efficiency on restorative, and maximize your technology. Make sure you never turn a patient away because you don't have a way to give them what they need or want.

Along those same lines, add more services: Invest in 3D cone beam scanning, like Galileos, so you can do bigger and more complex implant cases with much higher accuracy and better results. Learn do to Six-Month Smiles, or other new services. If you own a CEREC or other CAD/CAM technology, get more training so you can work faster—you only have your 30 hours per week to produce dentistry, so make the most of them. Train an assistant to do more of the CEREC steps, so you can work on more patients. If you don't have CAD/CAM yet, consider the fact that patients have less time than ever to leave work and come see you, so same day dentistry is even more appealing.

Most of all, take all emergencies. As more and more people who would normally see a dentist procrastinate, you are going to find real advantages in providing emergency care. And if you're open on a Saturday, you'll be amazed at the emergency business you could be doing. Use that tactic where you have a dedicated cell phone that one of your team members takes home every night to field emergency calls. Have them triage on the phone, and then you can see the patients that need your treatment.

Growing your practice through advertising is only effective when you don't waste the potential patients. Follow the rules in this chapter and your advertising will pay off well. Using the right words to help patients understand the care they need, then waiting for them to be ready to accept treatment, will yield the best long-term results. And speaking of words, in the next chapter we are going to explore the magical marketing power of using the right words in the right situations.

ACTION ITEMS:

1. Create a "new patient opening" policy for your appointment schedule.

2. Get every new patient in within 48 hours.

3. Eliminate procedures that prejudge patients' ability to pay or accept treatment.

4. Add new skills and services to broaden your appeal to patients and increase your daily production.

CHAPTER 17

WORD POWER:
SAYING THINGS
THE RIGHT WAY

If I've learned anything in business, it's that there is a right way to say almost anything. Used well, words can be magical. People can be put at ease, made to understand, be persuaded. There are also wrong ways to say a lot of things, and unfortunately, these are the phrases most commonly employed.

There are many practice consultants who can go through your procedures both in the front office and on the clinical side and tell you the best way to say and present things. For your convenience, I've listed many of them in Appendix II. What I'm going to do is give you some powerful examples of "success maximizers," phrases that in my experience are marketing magic. My recommendation would be to ideally use them word for word, or make them your own while sticking as close to the precise phrasing as possible.

Many staff members, and even more dentists, resist the idea of scripts. But if you appreciate that everything is marketing, why wouldn't you want to utilize the most effective words whenever possible? Why would you want to average down your results? Simply because you don't want to repeat yourself?

Let me use the example of Jerry Seinfeld. He will come up with the idea for a joke and hone it down to the precise wording that most effectively delivers that punchline. Then he will tell it *exactly that way* every single time he's on stage. He tells this joke about being in a movie theater: "We have an unwritten agreement with the theater owner that when we are finished consuming our snack, we open our hand." He doesn't say, "Throw it on the floor" or, "drop our trash." He very specifically says, "Open our hand." Can you see the precision, the uniqueness, the memorability of that phrase? It's perfect. And it's not just him, it's every successful comedian. You might think, "Isn't it boring to say it the same way over and over again?" Not if it works. In his case, it gets a laugh. In your case, it may get a new patient, put someone at ease or enable you to start a huge restorative case.

It's easy to resist using scripts. And it's even easier to get out of the habit of using them. But learning them by heart is important. Think about what that phrase means. "By heart" means you are learning the words as an actor does, by deciding what the character *feels* when he is saying the words. That means you empathize with the person you are talking to. When you are talking to a fearful patient on the phone, all you have to do is think about a situation where *you* might be fearful, and then say the words that will help them to take care of themselves.

When an actor is playing Hamlet and says, "To be or not to be, that is the question," he's feeling the despair of someone who is thinking of ending his own life. But he's not saying, "I wonder if I should commit suicide." The words Shakespeare chose are much more powerful for their subtlety, and much more memorable because of their unique phrasing. The actor understands the feeling behind the words, and has learned the line *by heart*.

Here is another very good example of the right words to say in a particularly difficult situation. As I got older, I found myself going to more and more funerals, but I would never know exactly what to say to the relatives of the deceased. I was fortunate enough to have a family friend who was a funeral director, and he taught me to say this: "I'm sorry that you lost your husband." Obviously, I change the name to fit the situation, but that's all I change. I say it exactly that way every time. And there is nothing insincere about it. I really mean it, and I've found a way to express it comfortably, without having to invent a new way of saying it every time.

Another example happened once when I was in a restaurant in San Mateo. The waiter brought rolls and butter, but he didn't just put them down on the table. He said, "Here are some rolls straight out of our oven, and our fresh-churned butter from a single Normandy cow." Now that's a masterful use of language to describe something simple. I ate five rolls.

Here, in no particular order, are some key marketing situations and the right words to say when faced with them. My advice is to pick one or two of these and try them. I think you will find they are extremely powerful, and you and your team will start using them over and over. Once you do that, they will become your own. First I will say it the wrong way—then the recommended way—sometimes the difference is subtle, but I hope you can see it.

ASKING FOR REFERRALS:

Let me first emphasize again that asking for referrals is an active process, not a passive one. The sign on your front desk is not enough. And I know dentists and team members don't want to sound desperate for patients, which is why you don't say it this way:

WRONG WAY: "We could sure use your help getting us patients. Please tell people about us." Or, worse, "If you find us any new patients, we're going to give you a nice gift." Or the worst way: not saying anything.

RIGHT WAY: "If you're happy with the care we've given you, we'd love to offer that same care to your friends and family if the need arises. Please feel free to recommend us to them." You are now communicating two wonderful things that people love to hear: "We like you," and "We have something nice that you can offer your friends—us!"

They might even say, "Oh, I didn't even realize you could handle new patients." Why would they say that, you might wonder? It's because if your office is busy, they see it in the same way that they see a busy medical practice. As you know, many of the best MDs, particularly in certain specialties like an Ob-Gyn, do not accept new patients. And many dermatologists are booked three months out. This is the model people are used to.

Even better, have a few special business cards that have an offer for new patients on the back, such as a free exam and cleaning, or whatever you're comfortable offering to referred patients. Give a couple of these to your patients when you ask them to refer you—not a whole stack of them, just two or three, otherwise they feel like now they're working for you for free. Say, "When you recommend a friend, we do this special offer for them, which you can see on the back. We don't do this for everyone, just friends and family of our patients." This makes them feel special, and gives them a card to hand to someone with a little incentive on the back. Every little bit helps to get people to take action.

ENCOURAGING CONSISTENT PREVENTIVE CARE:

WRONG WAY: "You really need to start coming in every four months. You're not coming in often enough." This sounds like you need money, or maybe that you just like sending people on a guilt trip. How about:

RIGHT WAY: "Did you know that the plaque in your mouth actually doubles every month? That means if you come in every seven months instead of every six, there will be twice as much plaque. We can really protect your gums and the cleanings will go even easier if you came in every four months. Can we schedule you for that?"

Now that's basically medically true, depending on all sorts of factors, but it's very easy to understand. The two advantages, protecting their gums and easier cleanings, are very clear, and you're recommending it for their benefit. The first time they come in for a cleaning after four months and it's nowhere near as uncomfortable as after eight months, they'll be sold on the concept. Do that with your whole practice, and you'll be amazed what tighter recall will do for your production.

INTRODUCING COMPREHENSIVE CARE:

WRONG WAY: "You've neglected yourself for a long time, so you need an awful lot of dental work done as soon as possible. Shall we get started?"

RIGHT WAY: "I can tell you what you're going to be doing 30 years from now." "Really?" the patient will say. "Yes, eating. Three times a day. Five if you're on a cruise ship. And you're going to want all your teeth to do it. That's where I come in." This introduction to a new smile is light, unique and completely to the point. Let it fly once and I guarantee you'll get tons of mileage out of it.

A STAFF MEMBER PRAISING THE DENTIST:

WRONG WAY: "Don't worry, the dentists here are usually very good."

RIGHT WAY: "You know, Dr. Wigwam is the best dentist in town, maybe one of the best in the state. I could work anywhere, but I work here because she's fantastic. I love being here. We love the patients here, but most of all, we're so proud of our doctor and the skills she has and the way she treats people. My whole family comes to her."

This could happen on a tour, or anytime chairside when the dentist is not around. All of the team members should be armed with this. If it's not true or they don't believe it, then either you need to get better or they need to quit. The dentist can't praise herself without sounding arrogant, but the whole team can sing her praises to a nearly absurd level, and it simply gives people reassurance that they've made the right choice with the practice. We all love reassurance when we're in a new or unfamiliar situation, especially where we have apprehension about what's going to happen (like say, the first visit to a dentist's office).

PEOPLE'S NAMES:

WRONG WAY: Don't use them.

RIGHT WAY: Use them whenever possible. As I mentioned in the loyalty tips, most practice software now allows you to put thumbnail pictures of patients with their file. If you haven't taken a photo of them for dental purposes, use a phone or a small digital computer camera that sits at the front desk and you can do a quick snapshot of them to put in the file, just so you recognize them the minute they walk in the door. They could even email you their favorite photo (the one they use on Facebook®, for example) right from their phone.

Everyone likes to hear their name. If you know they're coming in, greet them by name. Have everyone do it when they see them. Don't be shy. Shy is bad marketing. People love simple courtesy, and it's harder and harder to find. Make it easy to find in your office.

YOUR INITIAL PHONE GREETING:

WRONG WAY: "Doctor's office." Or worse, "Doctor's office, please hold." Even worse, "Drs. Ficklestein, Feinstein, Tabugabi, Green and Black's office. Can I help you?"

RIGHT WAY: "Happy Face Dental, this is Connie, I can help you." Notice Connie says, "I can help you," not, "Can I help you?" She is the one who can help you. Don't put people on hold the second they call. Put the person you're talking to on hold, or get someone else to pick up. If you have a complicated name or a series of names, don't call your dental practice that. You're not a law firm.

RESPONDING TO "WHY ARE YOU SO EXPENSIVE?":

WRONG WAY: "We're not that expensive. Other dentists charge even more." That is defensive, unpersuasive and doesn't answer the question.

RIGHT WAY: "With all the training that my staff and I get, and all the new technology we use to offer you the best, most comfort-conscious dentistry possible, I couldn't possibly charge any less. But isn't that the kind of dental care you want from me?"

Or you could say, "I'm very proud of our fees. We keep them as low as possible, considering the high quality of care our practice delivers every day."

RESPONDING TO A FEE DEMAND OVER THE PHONE:

WRONG WAY: "Okay, a root canal is $1,200."

There are several ways to address fees on the phone, mostly involving not trying to do a diagnosis over the phone and emphasizing the care and quality of the practice, as well as the concern the dentist would have about the caller's condition. But when the caller insists on a dollar amount, most front desk people fold. Here's what I would say instead:

RIGHT WAY: "It sounds like you're looking for the cheapest dentist office in town." If the patient agrees, say, "I have their number right here. Call them, and if you're not happy with the care that they give you, because low-cost dentistry is often not ideal, then come back and see us."

If the patient protests that they're looking for a reasonable price, not the worst dentist in town, you can follow with, "Well, our fees are very reasonable. What we offer is terrific dentistry.

Our dentist really cares about you, and I think you're really going to like it here. And, from what you've told me, the dentist would be very concerned about what's going on in your mouth. Once he sees you, he can figure out what needs to be done, and you have our promise that we'll discuss it with you and won't begin any treatment without getting your approval first. So, can you come in this afternoon at 2, or is 4 o'clock better for you?"

Or you could say, "I'm sure you could get your treatment done more cheaply, but having worked here for three years, I also know that you couldn't get it done any better."

Or, "We get the best training and use the highest quality labs and materials so we can get the best results. In our experience, nothing cheap is good, and nothing good is cheap. We think your body and your health should be looked at as a good long-term investment. Don't you agree?"

Don't diagnose over the phone. Sell care, not bargains. Focus on getting them in and letting them see what great dentistry can be, and why it's worth it.

THE 30-SECOND CASE PRESENTATION:

WRONG WAY: "Look, this is going to cost $25,000. I have lots of lab expenses with it, and I'll be using super-triple porcelain veneers and a Sirona® high-speed hand piece that I really enjoy using, and you'll look great after. Trust me."

RIGHT WAY: "I've received tons of training to do this exact procedure, I'm going to use the best materials available and you are going to be amazed at the difference your new smile is going to make in your life. Should we get started?"

This exact phrasing was taught to me by Dr. John Chaves, in Woodland Hills, California, whom I consider one of the best dentists in the country, and it works for him. Many dentists get bogged down in explaining the technical aspects of a restoration. The reality is, the patient probably doesn't really want to think about it too much, and if they do, they'll ask. I know several dentists who sell huge cases with essentially the type of presentation that I spell out here. They build trust first. The patient absolutely knows that the dentist cares about them, they appreciate that dentistry is a good investment, and all they have to decide is how to pay for it and when to start. It works.

If they still seem unsure, you can add this thought; "This is the same treatment I would recommend to my own brother-in-law" (or whoever might be an age/gender match). This is stronger than saying, "This is what I would do myself," because then they're thinking, "Sure, you're rich. You can afford it." When you associate it with someone that you care about, that sentiment transfers to them. It gives them the impression that you are recommending the procedure to benefit them, not yourself.

WHEN A PATIENT IS LEAVING BECAUSE OF INSURANCE:

You will lose patients because their insurance changed. It's going to happen, but this is one of the most critical times to say the right thing so that you improve your chances of getting the patient back someday. (I'm repeating this from Chapter 8 because I think it's so important.)

WRONG WAY: "We're sorry. We don't accept that insurance. They just don't pay enough."

RIGHT WAY: "We realize that cost is a factor in dentistry, and if you feel you need to leave the practice because your insurance changed, we completely understand. We're happy to transfer your records over to the next practice, and if you ever have questions about any treatment that they suggest, always feel free to call us and we'll be happy to give you our recommendation. And if your insurance changes to a plan we accept, or if you miss the care that we offer here, remember that you are always welcome back."

The last sentence is crucial, because what often happens is the person does get new insurance that you do accept, or they simply miss the level of care you provided and are now willing to make up the cost difference to go out of network—but they are reluctant to come back to your practice because they are embarrassed about leaving you because of money. They feel like a cheapskate. You want them to know that they are always welcome back, and that you do understand why they left.

WHEN YOU ARE EXPLAINING CAD/CAM LIKE CEREC:

WRONG WAY: "It has a 3D camera with a computerized lathe that builds teeth from porcelain blocks and was really expensive but we like it."

RIGHT WAY: "This is our *treatment accelerator*. We can now do crowns in a single visit, so you don't have to get a temporary put on , then come back in two weeks and get numb again to put the new crown on. It saves you time and gives you a beautiful porcelain crown that matches your natural teeth perfectly. Patients like it so much that we use it for fillings and onlays as well. We don't do amalgams or composites anymore, because CEREC restorations look much better and last much longer."

WHEN SOMEONE SAYS, "I COULD NEVER DO WHAT YOU DO ALL DAY!:

You will meet people who say rude and offensive things when you tell them you are a dentist. I hear it sometimes myself, because people think I'm a dentist. And even though they have fears about dentistry, I find the willingness to say thoughtless things to you unacceptable, and this would be my response to that remark.

WRONG WAY: (sheepishly) "Yeah, but you're probably going to need me someday."

RIGHT WAY: "What? Get people out of pain? Make them healthier? Improve their appearance and give them more self-confidence? Help me to understand what kind of person you are that you could never do that all day. Unfortunately, some of what I do makes people physically uncomfortable, and they're often scared, but I'm willing to make that sacrifice and even endure your dopey jokes and insults, because I believe in what I do. I think it's important. And I think you'd be hard-pressed to find a profession that does more for people's well-being and is less appreciated for it than mine."

You may not get to say it often, but when you do, I expect it will give the person something to think about.

AND FINALLY, A FEW REALLY POWERFUL WORDS:

"UPGRADE"

Everyone knows what that is, and anyone who's ever flown coach wants one. You can use this word to describe a number of the procedures that you offer. When presenting the option of CEREC restorations, you could say, "We can do a composite restoration for that tooth, and it will last several years and look similar to the natural tooth. However, we do offer an upgrade to the treatment, which is a CEREC restoration made with real porcelain. It will last much longer and match your other teeth perfectly. This upgrade will cost a bit more, but we can do it more quickly and in a single visit."

Or you could use it when explaining implants versus dentures—or veneers versus whitening. It's a great word, and people generally want to figure out if they can afford the upgrade.

"YET"

This word has some real emotional influence when used properly. It is particularly useful in getting patients to come in right away when they are calling with a tooth problem. Here is our fabulous fictitious appointment coordinator, Connie, using it to great advantage:

PATIENT: "I feel like I grind my teeth."

CONNIE: "Are you having headaches *yet?*"

PATIENT: "Not yet. Is that going to happen?"

CONNIE: "It might. You should really come in right away."

Or...

PATIENT: "My tooth is really throbbing."

CONNIE: "Are you having any shooting pains in your jaw *yet?*"

PATIENT: "Not yet. Is that next?"

CONNIE: "It could be. I wouldn't wait. Why don't you come in at 2?"

"Yet" creates a sense of urgency in the patient's mind, especially when they are minimizing their own symptoms to stay in avoidance mode. It is a very effective word for getting people to take action. Use it liberally!

"WHY NOW?"

When you have a patient who has come in after years of avoiding the dentist, ask them, "Why now? What's changed that has made you decide to come in?" Then listen very closely to the answer. It will lead you to what is most important to them, and your case presentation will flow very naturally when you understand their motivation.

I could fill a book just with the right scripts, but I wanted to give you some strong examples of how words can be your most powerful marketing tools. Talk to the experts and find out how to infuse the proper words into every situation.

"INVESTMENT"

I know treatment coordinators and dentists who are now abandoning the word "fee" and replacing it with the word "investment." It's a very subtle way of changing the patient's perception of the spending, and I really like it. Help the person focus on the idea that this is an investment in their body, not just some unexpected cost.

I hope you can now see how marketing permeates your entire practice, and why advertising alone cannot do the job. But how do you do effective advertising? That's what the next section is all about.

ACTION ITEMS:

1. Try incorporating one of these scripts each week.

2. Get some real practice management scripting from experts.

SECTION THREE:

REFINING
YOUR
ADVERTISING

CHAPTER 18

MARKETING IS
A PROFESSION

A few years ago, some friends of mine wanted to go sailing. They had rented two sailboats. My friend Gary looked at me and asked, "You can sail one of them, right?" I had been sailing before, so I thought, what is there to it? You move the sail this way, then that way, turn the rudder, tack left, tack right—simple. So I said, "Sure, I can sail."

Eight people climbed onto my boat, and eight people climbed onto Gary's boat. They took off out of the marina first. I started the small outboard engine, had people untie the boat and began to motor out of the harbor. My "crew," of course, had complete confidence in me and began to relax for a pleasure cruise. The main sail was already up, but unfortunately, I didn't realize that the boom was still tied down. As I tried to turn the boat out of its slip, the sail caught wind and pushed the boat straight across the marina toward the dock on the other side. No matter what I did with the rudder, the boat kept going straight.

The man running the boat rental place saw us and ran around the dock and grabbed the front of the boat before we crashed. "I thought you could sail," he exclaimed. I answered, "Well, I'm not a captain or anything." The truth was, I had been sailing a few times as a passenger, but that was the extent of my experience.

Now we needed a real captain, so I (naturally) went to the nearest bar and immediately found an old salt who was happy to do it for a case of beer. He jumped on board, sailed us out of the marina, and within 15 minutes caught up to the other boat. As we passed them, we cheered our able seaman on.

My point is this: Just because I had been on a sailboat didn't mean I knew how to sail. People seem to have this same confusion about advertising. They figure that because they've seen so much of it, they can easily do it themselves. Advertising is a profession. I've been doing it for 25 years and I still learn something new every day. It seems easy, because great advertising is supposed to look easy. It's not. It involves an array of skills—copywriting, art direction, cinematography, editing, media planning—all of which are full-time careers for people.

> "Let a professional do your advertising, while you focus on your marketing."

The fact is that advertising is the most rapidly changing form of communication in the world—and the Internet has accelerated the game drastically. It involves a set of skills that you couldn't possibly keep up with. Yet dentists try. They write their own ads, they build their own (horrible-looking) websites and they act as if because they've seen advertising, they know how to create it. Where did this skill set come from? You refer out your oral surgery, your endo and your perio, and you outsource all your lab work. You do that because you rely on the advanced skills of others in *your own profession!* Plus, you have a bookkeeper to do your expenses, a CPA to do your taxes and a financial planner to manage your portfolio. But somehow you are an instant creative director? Hmmm.

There is a reason major corporations like Coke, Sony and Toyota all use ad agencies—because it's worth it, and there is no way they could be as effective developing all their advertising internally. Good advertising is hard. But good advertising also gets a lot more results. Do you understand reach and frequency (the basics of advertising)? Or search engine optimization? Most dentists don't even know what these are, never mind how to excel at them. I spend hundreds of thousands of dollars a year to keep my company's websites up to date on website optimization, and I'm barely keeping up.

Getting professional help when you need to do something that is not within your skill set is not an arcane concept. You can make more money in dentistry than I can make in marketing. (Believe me, if I had the choice I would have gone to dental school.) Why would you try to become a part-time advertising expert? The amount of effort it takes to do that is not worth it. Get better at dentistry. Get *faster* at dentistry. You'll produce more, and you'll be happier.

A final note. Advertising isn't 100 percent. It is not an exact science, and there are no guarantees. But your dentistry probably isn't 100 percent perfect either, and neither is your dental lab's. However, just like with your lab, the way to improve your odds is to go with someone who has the skill, the experience and the reputation. Many dentists don't seem to grasp that their practice has its hands full just handling referrals properly. If you truly want to maximize your advertising results, get good at answering the phone and at getting patients in the door and accepting treatment. Focus on building the trust and respect of your patients and let someone else do your advertising. You'll cross that overhead threshold faster and you'll start making a serious profit margin—and the cost of outside advertising will be a good investment.

Notice I didn't say "expense." Good advertising is a good investment, just like dentistry. It is not an added expense, even though your accountant calls it that. It is the fuel that builds your practice. You can run on coal or you can run on rocket fuel—it's up to you.

Once you have the internal marketing aspects of your practice humming, get professional help to create and place your advertising and build your website. In the next chapter, I'll dive into the most important part of advertising for any business, which is accurately measuring the results.

ACTION ITEMS:

1. Honestly assess the time you spend doing your own advertising, and compare that to what you could earn doing dentistry, which of course would allow you to pay someone else to do it for you.

2. Get professional help to do your advertising. Find someone with a good reputation who has been around for a while and knows dentistry.

CHAPTER 19

TRACKING YOUR
ADVERTISING AND
BUDGETING

Here's how most dentists track the results of their advertising. They'll ask the appointment coordinator, "How's that ad campaign going?" She will answer, "It's great. We got a new patient yesterday," or, "It stinks. Nothing but losers and shoppers." Then the dentist will make an advertising decision accordingly. Unfortunately, this decision is not being made based on facts, but on anecdotes.

Anecdotes are not statistics. They are a reflection of the mood of your staff member at that moment. Relying on them is a perilous approach to tracking your advertising, because the negative information tends to outweigh the positive—human nature being what it is. Your front desk may complain about the direct mail patients and not even realize that you are working on a $20,000 case at the moment from that very ad. You need to systematically track your results to know what's working and what isn't.

Tracking is perhaps the most essential aspect of your advertising. Without it you're shooting, or rather, spending, in the dark. You have to know in detail how many patients each type of advertising is generating. This can easily be done within your software. Virtually every practice management software has a place to enter "referral source," and most will run a variety of reports that will tell you exactly how your advertising is working.

> "Tracking is perhaps the most essential aspect of your advertising."

If job one on the priority hierarchy is answering the phone, and job two is asking for referrals, then job three is making sure that you have a source for every single patient in the practice.

It's this simple: Without the source entered, you can't generate any statistical analysis of your advertising. But with the accurate source entered, you can look at it several ways. These are the monthly reports I recommend:

Patients per Referral Source: This should tell you what every medium or promotion brought in, in order of the total number of patients per source, disregarding what you spent on the medium. My feeling is that word of mouth should always be number one and, if it's not, you definitely need to work on the internal marketing of your practice because it means you're not effectively asking for referrals.

Initial Production, Sorted by Referral Source: This aggregates the total *initial* spending of patients for each referral source. This is not the whole story! Many dentists stop with this report, and make a decision based on this data. This just hints at what patients might eventually spend. You need a more complete picture.

Cumulative Production by Referral Source: This report and the next one really matter, because they tell you your true return on investment (ROI) for each referral source. The reason, of course, is that you're not going to do the majority of the production from each patient for several months, or even years. You want to know what the advertising is really yielding in terms of *lifetime* value of the referral. This report should include at least three years of results.

ROI for Each Referral Source Cumulatively: This is the real number to gauge your marketing expenditures. This number says, for example, that for each of the past five years you've spent $25,000 with 1-800-DENTIST and produced an average of $100,000 of cumulative production on those patients. That's an ROI of 4 to 1. If anything yields results like that, by the way, you should do it all day long. But there is still more to analyze.

Cost per Patient by Referral Source: Now you're getting down to some real numbers. This tells you, for example, that to get a patient in from the Yellow Pages costs $478 per patient in advertising cost. Now, it's important to note that none of your advertising campaigns will yield patients at the same cost. You are looking to have the cost per patient to be within a certain range. You also may have a great cost per patient in one medium, but you are limited as to what you can spend. Direct mail may be yielding five new patients a month, but it doesn't mean you can double the mailer size and get 10. You might still get five for twice the money.

Indirect Referral Production Reports: One of the most important series of reports is probably the hardest to generate, but it can be done. You may have to talk to your software consultant to have the report constructed. These reports measure secondary, or indirect, production. In other words, the production done on the patients referred to you by an existing patient, tracked back to the original referral source. Let's say you got a patient from your website, and they spent $200 in the first year. Then they referred three new patients to you—and those three patients spent a total of $7,500 to date. If your website cost per patient referral is $240, you might think this is a losing proposition, while in fact you've generated $7,700 that you would not have generated without the website.

Wouldn't you want to know that information? Wouldn't you want to base your decisions on that level of knowledge? I would hope so. Remember the case of the dentist in Chapter 11 who had not renewed the 1-800-DENTIST membership and was still yielding production from it four years later.

Did Not Appoint Report: You need a system to track the results regarding patients who never came in. (They called and inquired about the practice, but they decided either on the phone or later not to come in.) You should keep a separate record of this information. I don't know of any software that tracks this, so you need to create your own manual ledger for this, or a spreadsheet that someone maintains. This is going to tell you one or two things: First, how good your staff is at converting referrals, and second, which advertising brings in curious people—or perhaps even the wrong people. While I think you should try to get every patient in, obviously if you don't take State Aid patients, for example, and somehow the advertising you're doing is bringing in a bunch of them, you need to take a hard look at both the content of the ad and where it is being placed.

QUICK ANALYSIS SYSTEM

Sounds like a lot of reports, doesn't it? And, ideally, you should run them all. But most dentists I know barely know their production and profit for the year, let alone something as detailed as this. So I will propose an alternative rule of thumb to judge your advertising.

This method actually came from a dentist who has a number of 1-800-DENTIST memberships in various locations in Los Angeles. What he says is this: "For every membership, I'm going to get 150 referrals, and I'm going to turn those into roughly 100 patients—and one of those patients is going to pay for the whole membership for the entire year. The rest, in my mind, is gravy."

Simple really. If an advertising campaign gets one case that pays for it all, the rest is all upside. That's what it comes down to, because your business model is unique, and word of mouth is your largest source of new patients, and the true value of a patient is not realized for years or even decades. You can only be so precise. And, as I said, you are looking for a cost per patient range within which you can justify your ad spending, not an exact number.

Now let me answer three questions I get continually from dentists.

What should my cost per patient be in advertising?

You have to decide for yourself, but successful practices are typically willing to pay between $150 and $400 for a new patient. For cosmetic or implant cases, $500 to $600 is reasonable, and indeed should be expected. Getting patients below $150 would be great, but most likely this would be a fluke and hard to replicate.

What Return on Investment should I expect?

If you're only tracking direct production, you could still succeed with an ROI of two or three to one. I think most advertising programs should yield better than four to one, but that doesn't mean you can't build a practice with less—especially if you are great at generating word-of-mouth referrals. If you are accurately tracking *indirect* production, then I think a 5 to 1 ROI should be your baseline.

What should my advertising budget be?

I see this answer in three tiers:

Tier One: A startup practice with no patients. You should allocate at least $50,000 (and as much as $100,000) in advertising in the first 18-24 months. This is up-front spending to get a patient base. You need patients before you can generate word of mouth, and before you can get your production climbing at a steady rate. You need to calculate this into your startup costs, because if you spend most of your money on the facility, and you only have a small cushion to offset your cash flow short-fall in the first year, you won't have any money left to build a patient base with advertising. That means you'll need some seriously good signage and probably a slew of insurance plans.

Tier Two: An established practice grossing less than $600,000 (or whatever your contribution margin threshold is). At this point you should be spending 5 percent of your gross revenue on advertising.

Tier Three: Above $600,000, or above your contribution margin threshold. At this level you should be working your way up to allocating 8 percent of your gross revenue toward advertising, probably hitting that point when you reach $1.5 million.

Also, when you hit Tier Three, you should reserve 5 to 10 percent of your total advertising budget for experimentation. You'll be surprised what new approaches might yield good results. It's gambling money, so don't be upset if you lose it. You're trying to learn something. Education costs money.

Don't forget: Whatever you're spending, if you find you can't appoint new media-generated patients within 48 hours because you're booked too solidly, then it's time to start backing off the advertising. You'll start wasting more and more of the potential patients, and your ROI will get worse on all your advertising. You either need to add an associate or drop an insurance plan to create ways to earn more revenue per hour in the same workweek.

Once you have your team effectively tracking by entering every patient source and you've established an ad budget, you need to understand the two most important rules to have effective advertising. That's what the next chapter is about.

ACTION ITEMS:

1. Put it in your priority hierarchy to enter the source of every single patient into your practice management software.

2. Create a "Did Not Appoint" ledger to keep track of the referrals who were generated but did not turn into patients.

3. Based on your gross revenue, set an advertising budget for the year.

4. Run monthly reports that tell you how many patients you attracted from each source, and what the initial and cumulative production was for each source.

CHAPTER 20

THE KEY TO
SUCCESSFUL
ADVERTISING

Think about the last time you decided to buy a new car. Let's say you were looking for a new Lexus sedan. Suddenly, there are Lexus sedans everywhere—in every color, especially the colors you're thinking about. You also notice that there are a lot more Lexus commercials on TV. Of course, all that really happened is that you became aware of them. Your interest in Lexus suddenly emerged, and your change in awareness made you notice what had always been there. This is the most daunting part of all advertising: timing. Timing your message to appear when the potential customer is interested.

Timing is also the one aspect of advertising that is completely out of your control, simply because you cannot know when that interest will occur in any individual's life. The way advertisers solve this problem has been unchanged since the first ad was scrawled on a cave wall: repetition. You must repeat your message over and over again to your target audience, in hopes that some percentage of that audience will be interested at that moment.

A dentist recently told me that he tried television advertising in his town, but it didn't work. He tried for a *whole month*, he said. Then he stopped because he felt after a month of running the commercial, everyone in town should know about him. This couldn't be further from the truth. Ad agencies know that people don't even consciously perceive the message the first three times they hear it, and generally don't respond until the sixth time. And that's if they're interested. It is an advertising maxim that if you fall below a certain repetition threshold, you will get virtually no results. And that applies to every type of advertising that you do, from direct mail to the Internet. This applies to both the *number* of times your ads run, as well as the *length* of time that you run them.

Advertising is 99 percent invisible—or it might as well be. We are exposed to so many ads, so many logos, so many images, so many products. How could we consciously register even a tiny fraction of those? Most of the time, we only register the ones that dovetail with our interests at that exact second. Otherwise they go in one ear and out the other, or in one eye and out the other—or both. I'm not sure of the biology behind that, but you know what I mean.

Getting people's attention is the name of the game in advertising, and it isn't easy. Dr. Louis Malcmacher, whom I mentioned earlier, joined 1-800-DENTIST a few years ago in his Cleveland practice. Dr. Malcmacher practices what he preaches and has a very successful practice. He generates great word of mouth, he has a marvelous front desk and he also has excellent signage on a major street. After joining, he was treating a new patient and realized that she lived (and had grown up) only two miles from his office. So he asked her how she found out about him.

"Oh, I called 1-800-DENTIST."

He asked, "Well, haven't you ever seen the place?"

"No, I've lived here my whole life but I never noticed it before," she replied.

When Louis told me this story, he was still a bit in shock. She had probably driven by his office 1,000 times in her life without actually seeing it. It escaped her notice every day because it was not in her interest. She didn't care until she needed a dentist and then she remembered seeing a 1-800-DENTIST commercial on TV.

National advertisers are not running TV commercials constantly on several channels and backing them up with print ads and billboards and websites because they have money to burn. They do it because it works, and because they know they have only one choice to solve the timing problem: repetition. You have the same problem in your own practice, with new patients *and* with existing patients.

What this translates to is that you need to spend enough money in a medium to run the advertising enough times and for a long enough period to be effective. In my own experience—based on decades of advertising in cities all around the country—if I break this rule I will be throwing the money away.

To make this even more challenging, at the other end of the spectrum you can have a problem with spending *too much money* in too short a period. This is less likely to happen considering most dentists' limited budget, but in this case your results will quickly level off, and no amount of spending will increase them. This can happen with direct mail, on the Internet or in radio and television.

"Timing is the most important aspect of advertising, and it is completely out of your control."

To illustrate this, let me use a hypothetical example. As every medium in every city yields different results, please do not use these numbers as a true representation of advertising thresholds. Let's say I spend $4,000 a month on TV ads in Boogietown, USA, and my commercial runs once a week. I will get virtually no response. If I double it to $8,000, suddenly I break through that threshold and I will get 100 calls. It will continue in this ratio until I hit a certain point, say $20,000, at which point response will level off, and my cost per call will become increasingly higher. Do you see how I could be wasting money at either end of the spectrum? (See Figure 8.)

Figure 8

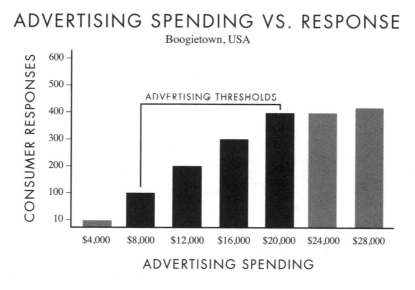

ADVERTISING SPENDING VS. RESPONSE
Boogietown, USA

This graph is for illustration purposes only. Numbers and city are fictional.

There is one more element you need to keep in mind when solving the timing problem, and that is making sure that your message gets to enough people each time it appears. You will only grab the attention of a small percentage of your audience with each repetition of your message. You need the audience to be large enough so that your response is significant enough. The concept of repetition in advertising is called *frequency*, and this concept of adequate audience size is called *reach*, which is shorthand for how many people your ad reaches each time. Just as you can have inadequate frequency, you can also have insufficient reach. Of course, your advertising message needs to be effective, but even the cleverest ad will fail if these interlocking keys are not factored in.

This is where the word "campaign" comes from in advertising. It is a constant battle for the mind of the consumer. Every advertiser is waging war with every other advertiser for people's attention. That means for your advertising to succeed, it needs to be a well-thought-out, well-coordinated and well-executed campaign. Are you capable of that? If not (and it's not likely you are), find someone who is.

"Frequency and reach solve the timing problem."

This same awareness challenge also occurs within your existing patient base. Ask yourself honestly, what percentage of your patients know everything that you offer in the practice? Do they all know you do Invisalign? Or implants? Or even whitening? Most dentists, when responding candidly, estimate that it is less than 10 percent. I would agree. If your internal marketing is working right, however, it should be 90 percent.

As I said before, I've talked to many dentists who've had long-time patients show up with a full set of veneers. Now that dentist gets to do prophys on that $25,000 smile for the next 15 years. The dentist will always say, "I told them I did cosmetics, or at least there was a brochure in the reception area. They should have known and asked me." Right.

This happens because you don't employ the basics of frequency and reach in your internal marketing. Because of the same timing issue, you need to tell your patients everything that you do over and over again. This is done with newsletters, email, your website and especially by your team. You have to stay at the top of their awareness so that whenever they think of their teeth, they think of you. And don't just tell patients about the procedures you think *they* might be a candidate for. Their parents may need implants, or their husband may need Invisalign. Don't try to figure out what they might need. Everyone knows other people with teeth. That's a big target audience. Put the word out about everything that you do. (PatientActivator, our internal marketing and digital communication program described in Appendix I, can do this for you with digital newsletters and email marketing campaigns.)

Solve this timing problem with consistent messaging to your patients and consistent advertising to your potential patient base, because if you don't, someone else in the neighborhood will.

In the next chapter, I'll give you my basic course in creating effective advertising (because I know you're probably going to try to do it yourself anyway!).

ACTION ITEMS:

1. Look at your advertising. Does it hit a large enough target audience clearly and often enough? If not, fix it.

2. Make sure your entire team knows everything the practice offers and can explain it clearly and simply. This is especially important if you have something unique, like CEREC, GALILEOS or a Picasso Diode Laser. Your whole team should be able to explain to patients why it benefits them, and that most dentists don't offer it yet. Have a little menu of your services and technology

with quick explanations that everyone can reference at the front desk.

3. Honestly assess how many of your patients know everything you do. Start communicating consistently with them in several ways, especially chairside. Consider PatientActivator, or a similar program.

4. Start sending print newsletters at least twice a year.

CHAPTER 21

ADVERTISING 101

Okay, I'm assuming you refuse to listen to me and you want to do all your own advertising. You'll want to know some basic rules. I'm not going to be able to teach you in one chapter what I've learned over 30 years (or even all of what I've learned *this* year), but I can tell you how to assess whether your advertising materials are likely to be effective. If you have decided to get professional help, these rules will serve as a guide for you to determine whether they are creating good advertising for you and placing it well.

YOUR TARGET AUDIENCE

The first thing to remember about advertising is this: People are not like you. They don't necessarily think like you; they don't watch what you watch on television; they don't read what you read or surf the websites you surf. So stop using yourself and your interests as the paradigm for all your advertising decisions. Advertising agencies spend a great deal of time understanding who your true consumers are and how they think, because your advertising message starts there. And of course, once the advertising is created, it has to be placed in a way that efficiently reaches that target audience, with as little waste as possible. Waste being what you are paying to promote your practice to people who are not your target audience.

In advertising you select the largest target audience, then you refine it to which segments of that target are most likely to become your customer. In dentistry, your primary target audience is women. Why? Because women make the overwhelming majority of medical appointments in this country. At 1-800-DENTIST, 70 percent of the callers are women, and most of the men who call were encouraged to do so by a woman.

"Women" is a pretty big target, but it falls into several categories, such as soccer moms, new college graduates, empty nesters and seniors. You do not appeal to all of them in the same way. They watch different TV shows, read different magazines and frequent different websites. In other words, not only are they not like you, they are not like each other.

If you recall, I mentioned the statistic that 16 percent of the population moves each year. That means two things: First, you're losing a certain number of patients every year and have no control over that loss. Second, some of these people are moving into your town, which makes new movers an excellent target market.

The challenge is that most people don't move and then immediately find a dentist. Even families can spend six months or a year in a new neighborhood before even thinking about finding a dentist. In our experience at 1-800-DENTIST, a "new mover," when it comes to dentistry, is someone who's moved in the past three years. New movers often turn into procrastinators and need to be motivated to get back on track with regular care.

As you can see, this is daunting. But the more you refine your messages to reach these different audiences, the more efficient your spending will be. Take the time to figure out whom you want to attract and then craft your advertising approaches accordingly.

YOUR ADVERTISING MESSAGE

> "Use the power of emotion to persuade, then give a rational reason to buy."

People buy emotionally. They buy from stores that they like being in. They buy products that they think will heighten their esteem. They buy cars because they are sexy, or they make them look sexy. But here is the human nature twist to it: They find a rational reason to justify their emotional choice. Because of this, good advertising uses the power of emotion to persuade people, and then it gives them a rational reason to buy.

How would that work in dental advertising? In a print ad, for example, you would use an attractive patient to draw their attention (the emotion), and then you would offer a whitening special (the rationale). Or you would explain that you can do complete restorations in a single visit, saving them time and inconvenience (the emotion), with your new CEREC technology, the only one in your neighborhood (the rationale).

MOTIVATE PEOPLE WITH YOUR MESSAGE

Here are some emotional motivators:

Fear is a very powerful motivator. (The longer you put off dentistry, the more it will hurt.)

Loss is a powerful motivator. (No one wants dentures.)

Happiness is a powerful motivator. (You'll look better and have more confidence with a new smile.)

Comfort is a powerful motivator. (The office offers IV sedation.)

Conformity is a powerful motivator. (*Your* teeth should be white and straight too!)

Uniqueness is a powerful motivator. (We do same-day restorations.)

Feeling important is a powerful motivator. (At this office, we treat everyone like family.)

Vanity is a powerful motivator. (If you don't believe me, just check the newsstands.)

THE LITMUS TEST FOR GOOD ADVERTISING

When looking at each piece of your advertising material, ask yourself these four things:

- Is it clear?
- Is it memorable?
- Is it honest?
- Is it believable?

All good advertising meets these standards, whether it is a radio spot, a TV commercial, a print ad or a website. Let's break them down.

Your message needs to be *clear*, because people are paying attention for about a fraction of a second. If they have to interpret your message, or decode the benefit to them, you've lost them. I'll say it again: If people have to figure out anything in your ad, they're gone.

Your message and the information in it must be *memorable*. Otherwise they have to act immediately or they will forget about you and your ad is wasted. Your name, phone number or web address, and whatever headline or words you use have to stick in their minds. I have built an entire business based almost entirely on the clarity and memorability of my phone number.

Your message has to be *honest* for two reasons. First, it's not legal to lie in your advertising, despite what people think. Second, if you do not honestly represent your service or yourself, it's going to catch up with you. You are in this for the long haul, not the quick sale. If you call yourself a high-tech office, but haven't bought a single piece of new technology in 10 years, you're not being honest. If you say you're a gentle, caring dentist, but don't have nitrous or IV sedation, the caring part doesn't ring true—it seems like you only care about patients' comfort unless there are costs involved.

Your message has to be *believable* because, even if it's honest, if it somehow seems incredible, then people won't respond. "Painless dentistry" is not believable (and usually not legal to say in most states) unless you explain that you are using air abrasion or a laser. Beware of over-promising. People's expectation of dentistry is low enough that if you can save them some time, some pain and some money, they are interested.

IT'S NOT ABOUT WHAT YOU DO, IT'S ABOUT WHAT THEY GET

Your ad message should tell potential patients about the benefit to them—not just explain what the technology or service is. This is a basic sales and promotion principle: Your message needs to be about benefits, not features.

For example, you *could* promote Invisalign by saying it uses clear, plastic retainers designed by space-age computers. Those are the features. Or you could say you offer invisible braces that are removable, feel more comfortable and work faster than metal braces. Now you've hit the benefits. You've told people that these braces are not visible, can be removed for convenience and are not painful—and the patient will complete treatment sooner. It's a great message (and therefore a great product to advertise) because the rational reasons are rolled right into the emotional ones.

QUALITY COMMUNICATES QUALITY

Cheap-looking advertising, poorly produced commercials or a confusing or visually unappealing website communicate something very negative about your practice. The reverse is also true. If you want to attract patients who can pay, give them good art direction, design and cinematography, great functionality and an attractive, easy-to-use interface on your website.

Look at the Super Bowl. These advertisers are spending $3.5 million to run a 30-second TV spot. What you perhaps don't realize is that the average Super Bowl commercial costs between $1 and $2 million just to *produce*. They know how good the spot has to look to compete, and spend accordingly.

Now I know you're not running Super Bowl ads. But think about those nights when you are sitting there watching cable, and after a few TV commercials from national brands, suddenly there is an ad for a local restaurant, and the difference in quality is immediately noticeable. It's almost visually offensive. You can tell they shot it with their home video camera, the sound is a little tinny, and the pictures of the food are kind of gross.

This is the reality with your advertising wherever it's going to appear: There will be professionally made advertising everywhere around your ad. You don't want to stand out because of low production value.

BE BRIEF AND TO THE POINT

Brevity is the soul of advertising, because you have fractions of a second to draw their attention. In a multi-media world, most of the time you are competing with several messages at the same time. Even in the Yellow Pages.

I say this to my creative staff all the time: Too much information is no information at all. The consumer needs to get the whole message fast. You can't tell them everything you want them to know in the ad. The ad's job is simply to get them to call. The rest of the work is done on the phone and by you. Remember, the ad is not going to give them an in-depth understanding of the procedures. It is meant to hit their main interest, and get them to respond.

FREQUENCY AND REACH

We discussed these key elements in the last chapter. You don't want to repeat yourself too often to one segment of your target audience, but you don't want to expose yourself to a larger audience too few times either.

Many businesses get drawn into these mistakes, either hitting too small an audience too often, or doing a huge splash to their entire target audience—but only doing it once. An example of the first would be buying time on a radio talk show every day for a month. Talk shows tend to have very loyal listeners, so you're over-saturating a small audience with the same message. You'll eventually just irritate them.

An example of the second would be sponsoring a big event that only occurs once a year. Or buying one TV spot in prime time, even if the price is good. Once is not frequency, no matter how big the audience is.

Either of these approaches will vaporize your media budget while providing nominal results. Keep them in balance—miscalculating this ratio of frequency and reach is a classic mistake. Here are a few more.

TYPICAL MISTAKES

MISTAKE #1: LISTING EVERYTHING YOU DO IN YOUR OFFICE ALL IN THE SAME AD.

There is a principle of perception called the *primacy/recency rule*. Essentially, it means that people, when presented with a list, remember the first thing and the last thing in a list and forget everything in between. You're looking for memorability, not forgetability. Also, you're going for brevity, and this is a classic example of too much information offered being no information transmitted. Avoid long lists.

MISTAKE #2: EGO ADVERTISING.

People don't care about you—they care about them. Putting your face in your ad may make you happy, but it probably doesn't sell dentistry (unless of course, you're a female dentist, in which case I would make it very clear that you *are* the dentist and not just an actress or model). You are probably not the one who should be acting in your commercials either. I know you're probably thinking, "Fred, weren't you in all your company's commercials for five years? Are *you* an egomaniac?" Well, I suppose I may be a bit of an egomaniac, but I've also had several years of acting training, as well as voice training, and I use a really good makeup artist. And I'm surrounded by a team of advertising professionals who are constantly measuring the effectiveness of those ads with my face in them. So if my ads weren't effective, I would take myself out of them in a second. I can boost my ego with a trophy wife instead. It's cheaper. (Actually, it's not, but you get my point.)

MISTAKE #3: AIMING FOR SOMEONE ELSE'S NEIGHBORHOOD.

I meet dentists all the time who want to draw patients from the upscale city that is "just a few miles away" from the town they are in. It's not likely to happen. Consumers tend to go to a dentist in either the neighborhood where they live or the one where they work. Directing your advertising beyond a reasonable radius because you believe the people there have more income is generally a waste of money. You drastically diminish the potential response. In other words, you're breaking the rule about target audiences by spending money trying to reach people who are much less likely to respond.

Also, people in upscale neighborhoods usually already have dentists. That narrows your true target audience even more. Attracting patients from Beverly Hills sounds great, but you can probably count the possible patients on one hand. You want people who *don't* have a dentist. The bigger the target, the bigger your response. Avoiders, neglecters and new movers that are within your neighborhood/radius—there's your audience. And one final thought: People seldom go downscale to their dentist. They usually go upscale from their neighborhood, or at least seek the same level. In other words, if you are trying to draw from a neighborhood that is more upscale than your office location, you're going to have a seriously diminished return on your advertising.

MISTAKE #4: PROMOTING BEYOND YOUR GEOGRAPHIC RADIUS.

This is different from mistake #3 in that you are starting with your office as the center of your radius, but you are blasting your message far beyond the distance people will typically travel. That radius, which in rural areas can be 30 miles or more, shrinks to about 5 to 10 miles in the suburbs, and less than 3 miles in urban areas. In New York City, it's more like 8 blocks.

This is the problem with broadcast advertising (radio and television). When you live in a city that is larger than about

400,000 people, the majority of people you are hitting with your message would not come to you even if your office were appealing to them. With broadcast, you pay for how many people you reach, so the farther it goes beyond your true target radius, the more money you're wasting. Cable TV might solve this in some cases. I'll talk more about that and various other advertising approaches in the next chapter.

ACTION ITEMS:

1. Scrutinize all your advertising and marketing materials. Are they clear, memorable, honest and believable? Do they use emotion to persuade and give rational reasons to act?

2. Determine whether your ads and website emphasize benefits or features. Do you list too many services in your ads?

3. Look at how your advertising is placed. Does it balance frequency and reach? Does it hit your true target audience, and does it work within your true target radius?

CHAPTER 22

ADVERTISING APPROACHES PART ONE: TRADITIONAL ADVERTISING

There are two questions to ask about any advertising approach: "Is it sustainable?" and "Is it scalable?" You want it to be sustainable so that, if it works, you can keep doing it and getting similar results. You don't want to have to spend your time finding new approaches to promote your practice every month. You don't have time for that.

You want it to be scalable because, again, if it's working, you want to increase your spending to get more results at roughly the same cost per new patient. Everything will reach a level of saturation eventually, but when you find a winner, you want to be able to step on the gas.

As I mentioned at the beginning of the book, my company has spent over half a billion dollars promoting 1-800-DENTIST.

We have tried every advertising medium available, and also done public relations, health fairs, sponsorships and more. And we track results fanatically—our software has the capability of telling us what is happening *minute by minute* in every city all across the country.

I've also spoken with many dentists and practice management consultants about which advertisements and promotions have worked for them—and which haven't. From all this, I've distilled my very personal, and sometimes very strong, opinion on every approach. As always, it's your tracking that will tell you what to stick with, what to increase and what to bail out on. And because of the radical changes brought on by the Internet, I've broken these approaches into two chapters: this one, where I cover traditional advertising, and the next chapter, where I dive into the Internet world.

DIRECT MAIL

Direct mail advertising has been the approach of many practices for decades, and it still can work if done well. If it's well-designed, uses high-quality printing and has a good message in it, direct mail typically yields between 0.1 and 0.5 percent results. (That means for every 1,000 pieces that go out, you should get 1 to 5 new patients.) This will vary based on factors that are unfortunately out of your control: how many other dentists are doing it, what other dental advertising is going on, the receptivity of your demographic to "junk mail" and the quantity of direct mail that each resident already receives.

The other problem is that direct mail is going to burn itself out in somewhere between six months and a year. Then you'll have to let your market "cool off" for another six months to a year. This is why it's critical to track your results closely—you want to know when to stop. This also makes direct mail less sustainable. You can't count on it month in and month out indefinitely, which means you'll need something else to drive new patients in during the dry months.

I particularly like direct mail for new movers, but with a different twist. As I said, when it comes to dentistry, a new mover means someone who moved to the area up to three years ago. Instead of buying the very expensive list of new movers, buy a "stale" list (three months old or more) for a lot less money, and then encourage them to stop procrastinating and come to your fine dental practice.

RADIO AND TV COMMERCIALS

Broadcast advertising can be very effective if you're in a town that's small enough. If you are in a city that's too large, the return will diminish because new patients won't go any great distance to your practice. (See Mistake #4 in the previous chapter.) The solution may be local cable, but very often they can't tell you how many people will be watching the shows you will be on. Whereas the major TV networks (ABC®, NBC®, CBS®, FOX®) have Nielsen ratings that tell them the size of the audience, cable stations estimate viewership based on subscribers—which is the equivalent of making up the number. As long as you look at it as a gamble, and you have some money to experiment with, give it a try. But try it for three months, not one. And make sure you have enough frequency each month.

Get someone to produce a good-looking commercial. Cheap really fails on TV. With HD video cameras, the cost of producing a TV commercial has come down considerably, but this is not a job for your nephew in film school. You will probably have to pay $20,000 or more for a good TV spot.

Radio is a lot cheaper to produce, usually around $2,000 per spot. The difficulty with radio is that promoting dentistry is what we call "a visual sell." That is, in dentistry we normally do a lot of our emotional persuasion by showing the positive results. So in radio, you either have to paint a vivid picture or give a heck of a good guilt trip. (We use both methods with 1-800-DENTIST.) However, if you have a special service that you want to offer—something specific that you do, like implants or no-prep veneers—it may work. Tell the listener what is new and why your practice is different.

YELLOW PAGES

In my opinion, Yellow Page ads, the old standby, have become gradually less and less reliable or cost effective. There is a massive migration away from the Yellow Pages to Internet search, especially when everyone can do it on their smart phones. It's a dying medium, and there are simply too many books and no way to determine which ones people are throwing away and which ones they're keeping, if any. If you have a good position in a book, and your tracking is showing good results, stick with it. Otherwise, I would generally avoid this medium. Yellow Pages companies are also moving into the Internet in a big way (so as not to become totally obsolete) so watch that closely. Right now they are offering it as a combination with an ad in the book.

The biggest negative with Yellow Pages is that you are committed for a year whether it yields results or not. And once the ad is printed, it's in the book for as long as people hold onto it, so if you move or change your phone number midway through the year, or even two years down the road, you're out of luck. It's also much harder to track because if you are in more than one book, people generally won't remember which one they found you in, so unless you're being very sophisticated and using a different trackable phone number for each ad you'll never know the results. And you know how I hate it when you can't track results.

If you are going to be in the Yellow Pages, go for the color in your ads, stay around 1/4 page in size, and don't clutter up the ad with too much information.

NEWSPAPERS

I don't recommend most newspaper advertising. The total subscriber number is meaningless (and ever-shrinking), because it tells you nothing about who actually sees your ad. Plus, their ads are generally disproportionately expensive. Neighborhood papers are better, in my mind, and worth testing. They tend to be read by more people, and target locally. If you can become a dentist who is regularly—and I do mean *regularly*—featured as the dental expert in the paper (see Public Relations below), then it would definitely be worth it, but track it closely. Don't get locked in for a year.

The entertainment-type weeklies that come out in most cities and towns every Thursday are much less effective. How do you rise above the clutter of the 40 other dentists advertising? I can't imagine how, except by offering deeper discounts than the next guy. Why play that game?

MAGAZINES

Obviously you're not going to advertise in *People*™ or *Newsweek*®, so what we are talking about are those local high-end consumer magazines. Some cosmetic dentists may be able to justify the cost of these ad pages, but I would say most dentists will end up losing. Being in them makes you seem expensive, so your target audience is narrowed, and you don't have a good shot at the real goldmine of patients: the avoiders and procrastinators.

VALPAK®, ETC.

I hate this kind of stuff. You show up in a stack of 100 other advertisers, and the only people who open them are those looking for a big discount. Experiment if you must, but do it with a jaundiced eye, and look very closely at not only the total patients but the total production from the mailers.

DISCOUNTS/PROMOTIONS

First of all, never call it a discount to your patients—call it a cash courtesy. But generally, you will need a promotion of some kind in most of your ads. This is going to amount to a discount on whitening, Invisalign or an initial exam and cleaning. The purpose is to expose them to your office, but herein lies the danger: As I've mentioned before, the patient who came to you for a discount will very likely leave you for a discount. They tend to be the least loyal. Once you've found them, you may struggle to keep them. I'd rather you promote yourself as a gentle, caring dentist with a great staff and the latest technology. That way, you are getting patients coming to you for the right reasons. Even so, you may have to have some offer to make your advertising produce, so test different ones and watch the production closely. If you get a ton of whitening patients in, but they never come back for any more dentistry, you know that whitening has saturated as a good patient draw. Try something else.

In the next chapter I'll discuss the online coupon world, including services like Groupon® and Living Social®, but much of the same thinking applies.

SPONSORSHIPS

Sponsoring Little League Baseball® teams or local events violates the reach and frequency rules. They either hit too small an audience over and over again, or they hit the whole audience once. If you do them, look at them as donations, not advertising.

PUBLIC RELATIONS

PR is an unusual thing because, although some dentists can be very good on camera or in public, most just aren't well-suited for that environment. Normal people are usually not telegenic and get nervous on camera. That doesn't make good television. Dentistry in general doesn't make good television or good radio, *Extreme Makeover*® notwithstanding, and that's been off the air for a while. If you're that person, great. But I prefer to recommend approaches that work for most dentists.

The most you can hope for is a regular article in a local newspaper—and this is worth going for if someone else isn't already doing it. Become a source to the neighborhood reporter working the health beat. Offer him a tour of your office and take him out to lunch to discuss the importance of oral health in relation to a person's overall health. The next time he's writing an article, he may think of you as a resource and call you for a quote, or even a bylined article. Over time, you may build a name for yourself in this way. But keep in mind that in any given area, only one or two dentists can share the spotlight. Most likely, there are hundreds practicing around you. It takes a continuous PR effort (or a PR firm for a $5,000 monthly retainer) to keep you in the public eye. Even then you might fail, and there are no refunds. And I consider most PR unsustainable, which is a basic requirement for me, as you know.

BUSINESS CARDS

Everyone in your office should have business cards and hand them out liberally. They are so simple, and yet so powerful. People stick them in their wallet or on the refrigerator and suddenly, a year later, you have a new patient. Need I mention that your website address should be listed on your cards? This is reason alone to have a website. If you hand someone a business card with no website address, they are going to think you're from the Stone Age. Now you should even put your Facebook Page username on your cards as well.

Here is a way to dial up the results of your business cards significantly: First of all, your team should be out there bragging about you. The key element of this trick (and also a way to save money on cards by not having to print individual ones) is to only have the dentist's name or the practice name on them. When the staff member hands out the card, have them tell the person, "We're a great office so we're really busy, but tell them I referred you and we will get you in right away." Then have her jot her name on the back of the card and hand it to the potential patient—personalized, memorable and trackable. It also works fine if they have personalized business cards, as long as they write a note on the back. (NOTE: Don't get glossy business cards. You can't write a note on them, which is what makes them valuable and personal.)

REFERRAL SERVICES

As you might expect, I'm partial to my own service, but it is not available to every practice. We screen dentists before we recommend them, and we only add dentists when we can support them with sufficient patient referrals (see "1-800-DENTIST Referral Service" in Appendix I). But the advantages are several. First, it's sustainable. Year in and year out, you should get results. And it's simple. You don't have to do anything except answer the phone really well, which you have to do anyway. It's our job to figure out how to give you as many leads as you can handle, using whatever combination of media works best. In addition, the callers are screened, so your appointment coordinator only answers calls from people who are most likely to be patients for your office (unlike all your other advertising, which sends every call directly to you).

There are other referral services, many of them strictly online listing services. Very few of them have a live call center, so it's up to you to turn that inquiry into a patient. That's asking a lot of your team, so I hope they're up to it. Scrutinize closely the results for any referral service and see if they are delivering what they promised. Also make sure your contract provides a way out if they don't fulfill their promise.

Ask for references from other dentists who have used their service. And if they are just sending the calls straight through to you without any screening, those leads are worth a lot less. Similarly, if they are just promising a certain number of views of your website, it's really hard to assess what that is worth. If it's cheap enough, give it a try, and track it closely.

Let me stress that there is no secret way to get hundreds of potential patient leads at $10 apiece. Anyone who promises that is not going to be around long enough to give you your money back. If it seems too good to be true, it is. And sadly, these services often start up and go out of business quickly, taking your money with them. I make it look easy, so a lot of people think they can do it too.

FOREIGN LANGUAGE MARKETING

Remember how I recommended speaking another language in your office? You'll need to jumpstart that with some advertising. This is a whole different ball game. You may want to use the local Hispanic or Korean newspaper, or you may want to advertise in the ethnic supermarkets. They also have language-specific Yellow Pages, and in this instance I would try those as well. Eventually word of mouth is where all the patients will come from, and you will need to do very little outside promotion.

TEAM MEMBERS AS BILLBOARDS

I said this earlier in the book, but I'll remind you that this is an advertising program, and one of the best expenditures in promotion. Everyone in your office should have a perfect smile. You want them to be able to recommend your dentistry personally, and be walking, talking examples of your professional skill. Restore every team member's smile who needs it.

DENTAL SEMINARS FOR LOCAL BUSINESSES

If you are starting a practice in a new area, one of the least-expensive promotions you can do is to offer a dental seminar to local businesses in the area. Most businesses over 100 employees regularly do seminars for their staff, usually to explain benefits such as the 401(k) plan or their health coverage, or for sexual harassment awareness and things like that. However, almost none of them take an in-depth approach to their employees' dental health. This is a great opportunity.

Contact the Human Resources department of the company and explain to them the high cost of untreated dentistry, reflected in absenteeism and lower productivity. Say that you are willing to do one-hour presentations and explain the value of taking care of their teeth, and also explain in detail how their dental benefits work, if they offer a plan. You might want to mention to the HR person the fact that 50 percent of the population over 35 has some level of gum disease, which means their employees' bodies are fighting infection every day, which could be contributing to their rate of absenteeism. This might pique their interest.

Of course, if you do this for a local business, you should make sure you accept the specific company's dental insurance and you should be able to answer questions about the coverage. But don't be discouraged if they don't have any dental insurance. They will still need the seminar and will still reap the benefit of their employees taking care of their teeth.

Put together your own PowerPoint® presentation explaining how to brush and floss, the connection between overall health and dental health, the risks of gum disease, the advantages of dental implants and anything else you want to talk about. Then answer questions and hand out toothbrushes and business cards. I'm willing to bet you'll get a big case each time you do this. Do it for as many businesses as you can. Then get back there on a regular basis and a lot of work should come your way thereafter.

By the way, if your toothbrushes don't have your name and phone number on them, or your website, go back to page 1.

NEWSLETTERS

A newsletter is an advertisement to your own patients. This is baseline marketing to me, just like a website. If you're not communicating what you do to your patients on a regular basis, then why would you bother advertising to new patients? Send patient newsletters quarterly—either by email or by regular mail. I believe that both ways are beneficial. In fact, I'm a big believer in print newsletters. There is considerable evidence that they get read, and they hang around the house for a while. Remember the whole repetition concept—this is the primary way you address the timing issue for your existing patient base. And typically one good case will cover the cost of print newsletters for the whole year. Just do it, I say.

Newsletters have reached a point where they can be very personalized and have great content for your patients. This is where you will need a good logo, and some good photography of the dentist, the team and the practice, and also good before-and-after photos of patients. These are the same materials you will need for your website, by the way.

Two quick words about photography and video of patients. Make sure you get a full release to use the photography in any medium. Most dentists realize they should get a release, but have your patients sign a form that permits use *in all media, including social media, in perpetuity,* otherwise you do not have any right to display the photo anywhere, particularly in your advertising and on your website. And photography of actual patient results is still one of the most persuasive ways to promote your dentistry. You can find a standard release form online with a quick Google search. Get the same release from your team members.

The second word is this: Use a good camera. Use good lighting. Take a picture of the patient's face, not just their teeth. Have a place in your office where you can take a photo of the patient against a neutral background, where the patient will look good and their teeth will show well. And of course, digital is the only way to go.

APPOINTMENT REMINDERS

This is one of the most neglected opportunities in dental marketing. A patient is about to come into your office and you are sending them a postcard with a cartoon on the front? Hey, we all need a good laugh, and Garfield® may be hilarious, but he doesn't sell dentistry. This is the perfect opportunity to tell patients about one of the services you offer. Take advantage of it. If you don't take your preventive care messages seriously, why should your patients? It's nice to be lighthearted, and I recommend it all through your practice, but the most successful dentists I know will take advantage of this opportunity to communicate something more about the treatments available to their patients at this opportune moment when they are about to come back into your office for recall. PatientActivator, our digital communication service, does this automatically through email and text reminders. It saves time so you can talk to the people you need to.

GUARANTEES

Guarantees are marketing tools. My assumption is that you will redo any dental treatment that was your fault at no charge. Many dentists even redo a case when the patient is at fault, having either damaged the restoration with bruxing or when their occlusion is off. Guess what? That's guaranteeing your work. Why not spell that out to your patients?

It doesn't have to be in writing. Simply state it verbally, but with an extremely important caveat: This is another gem that came to me from Dr. Mark Morin. He guarantees all his restorations for life. That's right, for life. All he asks of the patient to maintain this guarantee is for them to be consistent on their six month recall. Do you see the brilliance of this? Most likely, the patient will not be consistent, so it's really your option whether to fulfill the guarantee or not (and most likely you will—it's a loyalty builder to do so). But also, it motivates the patient to be consistent, and even gives your appointment coordinator or hygienist an extra tool when she is appointing them. She simply reminds them how important it is to make that hygiene appointment in order to keep their guarantee. It works.

BE AWARE OF HIDDEN MARKETING COSTS

A marketing cost is every expense, implicit or explicit, that is involved in generating production. This includes a lot more than just what you spend on advertising. I'm not saying you shouldn't have these hidden expenses—you should. But I wanted to shed some light on some of the less-obvious examples.

1. *Insurance.* Accepting any dental insurance plan that is not an indemnity plan is a marketing expense. Essentially, you are offering a permanent discount on your treatment. The patient doesn't experience it as a discount, but you do. If you are accepting 80 percent of your normal fees on the plan, that's a 20 percent discount—and that amount is essentially an ongoing marketing cost for the life of that patient in your practice.

2. *Promotional discounts.* Let's say you run an ad with a whitening promotion—$100 less than you usually charge—and your tracking tells you that it cost you an average of $200 in advertising to get each new patient in from that promotion. Can you see that the patient actually cost you $300? You have to add the discount to your cost per patient. I would say it's still worth it if the patient stays with you for more care, but

if they don't, that's expensive. Track your promotions closely, and calculate the discount into the cost of getting the patient.

3. *Keeping up with technology.* Sometimes you need new technology to offer the highest standard of care. Sometimes you want it to make your life easier. Sometimes you want it to take advantage of what patients are asking for. And sometimes it's some combination of all three. Either way, implicit in your technology is a marketing cost, and you should look at it that way. Taking an Invisalign or an implant course in order to be able to offer that treatment has a marketing aspect to it. And it should.

I believe that if a dentist does not keep up with the latest demands from consumers, and doesn't upgrade his technology to offer the best possible care, then that dentist is going to gradually watch his practice disintegrate until he has nothing left to sell upon retirement. The days of practicing the dentistry you learned in dental school for your entire career are long gone.

When you are evaluating technology investments, don't just look at what the equipment will cost and how much money it may save you in time or material. Look at what it may get you with a marketing advantage, and purchase accordingly.

And remember my tip from Chapter 19. If one patient comes in who spends enough to cover the budget for a particular advertising approach, stick with it. You are really using advertising to attract patients who can lead you to word-of-mouth patients, so all the program has to do is pay for itself.

I hope this chapter helps you to make some better advertising decisions, and I hope this section has given you a better understanding of how involved advertising is, and will allow you to formulate a plan to maximize your advertising and grow your practice to great heights. In the next chapter, I'll add the critical layer of digital marketing and advertising.

CHAPTER 23

ADVERTISING APPROACHES PART TWO: THE INTERNET WORLD

In this chapter I'm going to cover everything in the online universe for your practice, from Facebook to Google; from online reviews to text messages; and everything in between. The fact that I'm putting this information in a book almost guarantees that some of it will be obsolete by the time you read it. The Internet environment is in constant flux, with new players and possibilities appearing all the time, and others falling by the wayside. But the digital world has its own rules, and many remain fairly constant.

First, you have to accept that the digital world is here, affecting every aspect of business. Pretending it doesn't involve you or your patients is practicing what I call "ostrich dentistry," ignoring the changes around you in the hope that they will not have any effect on you. Ostrich dentistry is not going to fly anymore, if you'll pardon the pun.

These are the facts: 25 percent of the population no longer has a landline phone; There are more cell phones than people in this country, and more than half of those phones are smart phones with Internet access; There are now more Internet searches done on mobile phones than on computers. That's a big shift. And free WiFi is showing up everywhere to make this even easier and faster. When most phones are 4G, the searches will be even faster still.

Just as you need to adapt to new technologies, it's also time to go digital in your office. It's the way the world is going and you need to get ahead of the curve. Patients will want to fill out the intake forms online before they come into the office. They will want to make and confirm appointments by email, or even directly on your website. This will make your life easier and cheaper. Get broadband Internet access and WiFi in your office and be prepared to integrate online activity more and more into your practice, because people will start to demand it. Don't be afraid that your team will waste the day away surfing the Internet. Assuming you've already fired the C-players, as I recommended in Chapter 14, you won't have to worry about that. Your A-players will set the tone and keep the Web surfing professional.

This digital revolution will affect every aspect of your business operation, not just your advertising and marketing. Texting is a perfect example.

TEXTING

There has been no more rapid adoption of a new communication modality than the use of text messaging on mobile phones. Virtually non-existent in 2001, there are now five times as many text messages sent as phone calls made. People use texting because it's incredibly efficient, and once they adapt it, they seldom check their voicemail and many don't even answer their phone. (If you have a teenager, you know that's true.) It has become the most popular method of communication besides face-to-face conversation. More than 80 percent of cell phone owners use text messaging. And 31 percent prefer it to a phone call.[15] As an aside, the prime minister of Finland, Matti Vanhanen, made front page news in 2006 when he supposedly broke up with his girlfriend by texting her. Now that's cold. But it's pretty cold in Finland anyway.

So how does this relate to your practice? Beautifully. It's possible to use texting to confirm appointments, send birthday greetings and even do last-minute reminders of patients' appointments, so that they don't forget. Our PatientActivator product does this automatically, as do several other applications, and it works directly with your practice management software. The value of this is that your front desk now has time to talk to the people who actually need a telephone conversation. In other words, your team doesn't waste three calls back and forth trying to confirm an appointment when an automatic text message can do the same thing and require no time at all. Perhaps most important is that many patients *prefer* to be reminded this way. And there's one more bonus, and this is true of all your digital communications: Your patients will view you as a modern, high-tech practice.

Texting used to cost people money on a per-text basis, but more and more people have a universal data plan.

CELL PHONE NUMBERS

To be able to text your patients, you must have their cell phone numbers. It's also often the best number to use when confirming appointments because you are getting directly to the person wherever they are, rather than to their home answering machine. As I mentioned above, at least 25 percent of the population no longer has a home phone, and this will continue to increase. Even though I still have a home phone and an answering machine, I no longer check the answering machine for messages. If people want to find me they call my cell—or they text me.

EMAIL

The greatest invention in marketing in a hundred years is email. First of all, it's free. That's hard to beat. But even more, it carries its own urgency. New mail arrives at the top of a list, which creates a sense of priority even if there is no real priority to it. I'm not talking about email blasting to strangers here; I'm talking about emailing your own patients—on a regular basis.

In my experience, the average office has 5-10 percent of the email addresses for their patients. But more than 95 percent of the population has one at this point[16], and half of them check it daily.[17] Collecting email addresses is something that your staff needs to be diligent about—asking every time a patient comes in, "Do we have your current email address? Do we have all your email addresses? Which one do you use the most?" No patient should leave the office without being asked for her email address. And get one for each family member. Make it standard operating procedure.

There are two ideal uses for email in your practice. First, as I mentioned earlier, appointment reminders and confirmations. There are several digital applications that work with your practice management software to do this, including ours, PatientActivator. They are all good products (mine's the best, of course!) and the only real mistake is to not use any of them. They are phenomenal time savers. And many patients prefer a text or email to a phone call.

The second use is to do email marketing to your current patients. Remember the key dictum of marketing: Tell your customer over and over what it is you do and why they should want it. That's what you can do with email. And it costs you nothing—it's part of these applications. And most have pre-made marketing campaigns that you can customize and send with a few clicks.

Email is simply a fantastic medium to communicate with your patients, to send them information about the services that you offer, or even just to tell them what kind of electric toothbrush you recommend. The purpose is to stay top of mind in their awareness. It's what we in marketing call a *touch*, where you bring yourself in contact with your customer non-intrusively, and helpfully, on a consistent basis.

EMAIL SOLICITATION FOR NEW PATIENTS

There are some services that will do massive email campaigns for you to attract new patients. They have lists of people's emails, and often have permission to email them. I can't recommend these email promotions (or email blasts, as they are often called) as a method of attracting new patients. Too many people have spam blockers on their inboxes, so your ad only reaches an indeterminate number of them. This means you don't know what you're paying for in terms of true audience size and composition—and I hate that. I don't believe you could ever cost-effectively generate new patients this way.

YOUR WEBSITE

Your website has become the cornerstone of your practice marketing. Even if you do direct mail, you need to have your website listed. We've found that even when a friend recommends a dentist, people will still check the practice's website before calling. It is one of the best ways to promote your practice, and it is the most robust brochure you could possibly ask for, with the potential for unlimited content—including detailed photography and even video. Bear in mind that 80 percent of the American population now uses the Internet at least once a month, and that will only increase to the point where most people are using it all day long. However, I cannot stress this next point strongly enough: You should not build your own website, no matter how easy it seems.

The power of your website will be in how well it is "optimized." This is a fairly new term in advertising, and refers to how search engines like Google™, Yahoo®, Bing® and others will categorize your website and the information in it. In other words, do they consider your website relevant enough to present when someone searches for certain words, such as "dentist Pittsburgh" or "cosmetic dentist 90210." Whenever possible, you want your office to come up on the first page of results *naturally*, which is to say, you're not *paying* to come up in the search.

This optimization issue is why you can no longer build your own website. You cannot possibly stay current on what is required to satisfy the systems these search engines have for categorizing your site. The methods of categorization change all the time, how they determine what is relevant is not easily determined and the search engines do not necessarily disclose what their criteria are. In short, you need professional help. As I've mentioned, at 1-800-DENTIST, we spend hundreds of thousands of dollars a year to keep up with search engine optimization, or SEO, as you will hear it referred to. And we can barely keep up. Have a website designer build you a site and make sure it is someone who can optimize it. You need a company that does websites for dentists—a lot of them—and has been doing it for a while.

If you already have a website and it hasn't changed in a couple of years, it's time to build a new one. If you don't have a site at all, get started on one *right now*. It doesn't need to be perfect. It needs to be up and running. You can perfect it as you go. Every day more dentists are adding their websites to the World Wide Web, and you don't want to be the last one to show up at that party. Many dentists tell me that they've been planning to get their website up for a year, but just can't get it together. It should take no more than a couple of hours to assemble the information necessary—maybe even less. Get on it.

Also, it's important to now have a *dynamic* website. This adjective means something specific in the Internet world. It means a website where you can change certain content easily yourself without using a webmaster. This is because search engines are looking for websites with a steady flow of new content posted. You should be able to put up new photos, videos, and especially reviews and testimonials from patients so that your website is changing all the time. The search engines do not like static content, and tend to ignore sites that haven't changed in several months. We realized that this has become so critical that we now build websites for dental practices. (See information about our WebDirector product in Appendix I.)

Websites also need to be able to accept content automatically. Digital communication applications like PatientActivator solicit reviews from your patients, and you can post these to your website, which is a huge benefit. Once you have your dynamic website, with ever-changing content you should also expect to do major design modifications to it every 18-24 months. Keeping up with the current levels of optimization and design demands is almost as important as having the website itself.

Websites also need to automatically adapt to whatever device or browser they are being viewed on. The problem with static and custom sites is that your webmaster needs to update them each time Safari or Internet Explorer updates their program.

And they usually want to be paid for this. And also, if you have Flash animation in your website, it no longer plays on Apple products. That's a big problem with a lot of websites that are more than two years old.

In particular, your website needs to completely reformat when viewed on a mobile device. It should not be a shrunken-down version of what appears on a computer. That annoys people and they move on. They should only need to scroll down to see more information, not have to move side-to-side. It needs to have a simple display, with buttons for your phone number, directions, and an option to request an appointment at the top. These are essential. And everything else isn't.

And this is key to remember about the digital consumer: They are making judgments about the quality of your dentistry based on the quality of your website. I understand that these two things are unrelated, but don't expect consumers to behave rationally. They are using all sorts of irrelevant clues to decide if they want to come to your office. Accept it, and know that your website needs a clean, modern look that loads fast and plays properly on every device.

The search engines no longer only care about what is in your website. They are looking everywhere else on the Internet for mentions of your practice: social media sites like Facebook and LinkedIn, online reviews, your blog and other directory sites. And the latest elements that they are looking for are links to your website from other local businesses. So what you should be doing is offering to list the websites of local businesses in your website, on the second or third page, and in return ask them to do that for you. Ask all the specialists that you refer to (or GP's if you are a specialist) as well as chiropractors, hair salons, trainers and anyone else you do business with locally. It will benefit both of you each time. Remember, most search results on mobile devices are based locally (because Google can tell where the phone is at that moment). Why is this important? Because 60 percent of searches now begin on smart phones. That's a big shift right there.

> **Consumers are making judgments about the quality of your dentistry based on your website.**

You should get new patients from your website, but how many depends entirely upon how many other dentists have websites in your area and how well your site is optimized. You will sometimes hear dentists bragging that they get 50-60 new patients a month from their website. This generally means that it happened once (because dentists don't really track results, they track staff anecdotes). But I also believe that in most cities, those days are gone, or soon will be. Eventually every dentist is going to have a website. It will not be mathematically possible for every dentist in the U.S. to get 20 or 30 new patients every month from their website. Those who were there first, with the best websites, will reap the majority of the advantage, but even their advantage will diminish. You will also encounter businesses that will promise you that your website will show up on the first page of a Google search, because they are the masters of search engine optimization. But that is no longer possible. Google uses 400-800 bits of information to decide if your website is relevant, and it will even change the results for the searcher based on their previous search behavior. So no one can guarantee first-page results. You're being lied to. Run.

Bear in mind that your website is incredibly useful for your existing patient base, too. They can get information about you and recommend you more easily to their friends. And more often than not, when your patient recommends you to someone, that person will check out your website before they call you. You can also direct your patients to your website with emails about new services and technology that you have in the practice.

Lastly, depending on the focus of your practice, you should consider having more than one website. If you do both general dentistry and a significant amount of implants, those are two different target audiences. Create two sites, and target each one accordingly.

BUYING KEYWORDS

This is called "paid search," which is exactly what it sounds like. You are paying to get a (tiny) ad for your practice to come up on the first page of search engine results. Google also currently has something called Google+ Local, which allows you to come up in a map of the immediate geographic search area. Your Google listing is free, and then there are paid options beyond the basic listing. In any case, with paid search you are paying every time someone clicks on your ad, which transfers the consumer to your website. As you can imagine, this is still a long way from the person becoming a patient. You can set a monthly budget for how many clicks you buy, and you are in essence bidding for a position on that first page of the search.

For example, you can say you want to bid a maximum of $3 every time someone searches for "Dallas dentist." Then you won't pay more than $3 for that click, but if people are bidding more than you, your ad won't appear. Using the Google keyword tool, you can see what the current bid ranges for that keyword are. Then you tell them that you want to spend a maximum of $600 in the month. You'll get clicks until this money runs out, and then your ad will no longer come up until the next month. You will get a report on what you paid per click, on average, how many clicks there were, and what your average position was on the page.

When you set yourself up on Google Places, which I describe below, you can also set up a Google AdWords account and tell them which words you want to bid on. You can also pay to have your practice ad come up when the local map comes up. Of course, once half the dentists in your area have a Google Places account, the map will get crowded and you won't stand out unless you pay to be featured. This is similar to how the Yellow Pages work now, and I'm afraid it's heading in the direction of the same level of clutter.

With keywords, the bidding is becoming more competitive every year, especially for the most desirable keywords like "cosmetic dentist" and "dental implants." Some dentists are willing to pay $25 a click for these keywords so that they will come up in the first position. They've obviously determined that it's worth it and they've undoubtedly created a highly effective website so they can capture as many patients as possible. You want to be paying more like $1 to $3 per click, and you should expect that it will take between 50-150 clicks to get a real patient in the door.

By the way, the #1 paid position is overrated. Coming up in the second or third position is fine. Not only will you often pay too much to be first, there's an interesting phenomenon whereby Internet users will frequently click on the first paid ad and then go back and click on the second. More often than not, they forget the first website and use the second or third. Your goal is to show up on the first page. Also, remember that you are actually putting in a bid without really knowing what the position will be. (The search engines have factors beyond price to determine who comes up in what order.) You are telling them what your maximum bid would be, and they put that against all the other bidders, and you end up where you end up—first, second, fifth—and you are charged accordingly. The lower your maximum bid, the lower your position is likely to be, and the greater the likelihood that they will charge you the maximum bid amount. Complicated? Definitely.

You can also expect between 10-20 percent false clicks in any given month, or click fraud, as it's sometimes called. In my experience, Google doesn't like to admit that there is click fraud, but they will acknowledge "click discrepancies" (it's all about the right words, remember?). You will have people who have no intention of ever using you looking at your website and clicking your ads. There is almost nothing you can do about it—it's the cost of doing business.

The same purchasing of clicks and keywords can also be done on Yahoo and Bing. Though Google is the biggest player, each of these search engines has tens of millions of users, and it makes sense to spread some of your money around to different sites. And though a lot of what I'm telling you is true now, Internet marketing is the ultimate moving target—systems will change, new services will emerge and it will get more and more complicated. It's a game you have to enter, but I hope you can see you're probably going to need help.

ONLINE COUPONS: GROUPON, LIVING SOCIAL ET AL

For the most part these services are being restricted by dental societies, because it looks a lot like fee splitting (and often is exactly that). I believe the era of usability of these services has passed for dentistry, but if you decide to try one of them, go in with your eyes open.

Here are the problems:

1. Your front desk is going to be overwhelmed by calls, unless you staff to prepare for it, because most calls will happen the day of the deal;

2. Many of the patients who do show up are one-time users. This is particularly true with a whitening offer. Even with an initial exam offer, some patients will even ask for the x-rays after the visit to bring back to their own dentist;

3. Your own patients may see the deal and ask for the same price—that can get tricky to deal with;

4. You cannot do these offers very often, as way more dentists want to do them than Groupon or other services are willing to accommodate in any given month. That means even if it works, you'd be lucky to do it twice a year.

Personally, I am not fond of these services. I think they commoditize dentistry even more, and I think they will become the bane of small businesses as more and more people chase deals and change providers, and customer loyalty becomes a thing of the past. And generally, as I mentioned before, I don't like patients who came to you because of a discount.

ZOCDOC®

This is a fairly unique service in that you pay a flat monthly fee, around $300, to have your practice listed along with open appointments in your schedule that someone can come to the site and sign up for. It's not available in all cities, but it is expanding. Most dentists are reluctant to put their appointments up, but those that are trying it are not finding it risky to do so. The service is for all of health care as well, not just dentistry, and I think it works better for the physician world than it does for dentistry. When people are looking for a urologist, for example, they want one that accepts their insurance and has an appointment available. That's it. When they're looking for a dentist, insurance is only part of it. The experience of visiting that dentist is critical for most people, and so just because the dentist has an appointment available does not mean people are going to jump at the opportunity

AD WORD RESELLERS

There are several companies out there offering to do your Google Adword buying and planning for you. If you find this too daunting to do yourself, then understand that if you use these services, they are doing it for a profit. That means less of your money will go into the bidding for keywords than if you do it yourself. I'm not against it, as I think your time is valuable, but the keyword choices are not so complicated that your office manager could not do this and monitor the results herself. Again, if you're tracking the results and it pays off with little involvement on your part, it's worth doing. But you need to monitor their results continually because they may diminish over time.

FACEBOOK, GOOGLE+, TWITTER AND MORE

Social media is not a fad anymore. People are spending as much time on Facebook as they are watching television, and often doing both at the same time. You cannot ignore it anymore. Social media, quite simply, is the new word of mouth. It is going to require a specific strategy for a dental practice. I'll try to go through each of the important sites in detail, and help you prioritize your efforts. It may seem like a lot of crazy stuff to be involved in, but the strategy is fairly simple: The more places you are out there on the Internet with accurate, relevant, interesting content, the more likely you will come up on a natural (free) search on Google, Yahoo, et al. In other words, it's worth the effort.

Facebook is the monster out there. Compared to anything else in the social media world, nothing else comes close in terms of time spent and the number of real users. Just to give you an idea, 28 percent of 18-34 year-olds check Facebook *before they get out of bed!*[18] Facebook has radically changed how people interact with the world. And it has become a way that people learn about businesses, services and products from their friends, and their friends' friends. And it has evolved considerably into a marketing platform.

Also, women post four times as much as men. In other words, your target audience is extremely active on Facebook. For the dentist, there are two different aspects to the site: your personal profile and your business fan page. First, though less important, you need a personal page with a photo (or several photos) and a good description of yourself and your interests. You should also add updates on a regular basis. Be yourself on your Facebook profile. Don't be a self-promoter. Its purpose is to humanize you, and trying to hustle business in your profile defeats the purpose. Remember, you are doing the personal profile mostly to become familiar with the medium.

However, on the *business* side, your practice needs a *fan page* on Facebook. This is different from your personal profile. It truly is a business page where you can post videos of yourself and your practice, before-and-after photos, advanced training and services, and various other promotional items. It's where you want people to go to find out about your practice, and it's especially important when your patients on Facebook recommend you.

This is important to remember: Facebook is a closed system on the *personal* profile side, which means the search engines cannot look at the information and wall posts on personal profiles. However, and this is critical to keep in mind, the search engines do look at all the content on Facebook fan pages, and this adds to your SEO.

There is one more reason why active Facebook participation has become essential for a practice. In 2013, Facebook created something called Graph Search, which essentially allows someone to search for any sort of content on Facebook. Previously, if someone wanted to know what dentists their friends liked, they would have to post on their own wall and ask, and hope that some of their friends responded. Now, they can do a search that is almost identical to going on Google, and ask any sort of question and get results.

For example, if someone wanted to know what dentists their friends have been to, they would just search, "Dentists my friends go to" and the results would instantly appear. They can open the dentists' fan pages and read what everyone has posted. A person can now also search the content of the posts, and will get results. This radically changes the potency of Facebook from a marketing standpoint, and it's why I consider it so urgent to get involved.

So these are the steps:

1. Create a fan page for your practice. Use a good panoramic photo, usually of the team, but it could be anything that promotes the practice well. Someone in the office already knows how to do this by the way, so ask them for help.

2. Make it a habit, and even use some small signs at the desk, to ask people to "Like" your Facebook page (you can also do this with email through PatientActivator or a similar application.) Also, ask them to "check in." This is another trend that is exploding. Some people, wherever they go, check in to that location on Facebook. Some have even done it at your practice without you even knowing or having a page. It's based on your location, and they do it on their cell phones. This pays off in a Graph Search and also because Google counts the check-ins, and it counts toward your relevance.

3. Post on a regular basis, at least twice a week. More importantly, encourage your patients to post. They can put photos of themselves, even make a short testimonial video, or just say how they feel about the practice. This is gold from a social media standpoint.

4. Make it someone's daily job—not the dentist, ideally—to check Facebook and respond to any posts. It is absolutely rude on social media to let a post that a patient has made sit there without a response. If a patient posts, "I always love coming here. I always feel bet-

ter when my teeth are clean," then you should respond with something along the lines of, "So good to see you today, Jenny! You always brighten our day!" This gives people a sense of the practice experience in a very powerful way. This employee should also be responsible for consistently putting up new posts.

5. Try some promotions. (Holiday whitening specials, new patient specials, free implant consultations, things like that. Or even contests to get people to like your page.) Go to www.allfacebook.com to figure out how to do this the best way.

So what do you post? This is the question I get all the time. I know it seems challenging, but let me first tell you what *not* to post. Don't post clinical content, like how people should love Invisalign or floss a certain way. Facebook is where people can find out what the experience of being in your practice is like. Remember my main point of this book, which is that they can't gauge your clinical skills, but they can assess the experience easily, and that's what they go by.

So post fun stuff: pictures of team members, favorite patients, charities you're involved in, events going on in your town. It will become a habit to develop these posts, and your team can come up with them. It just takes a little focus. And the more you get patients to post, the more you get the content you're really looking for.

Also, don't be concerned on Facebook if someone posts something negative about you or your practice. The beauty of Facebook is *you can delete anything anyone posts on your page.* So don't be afraid of what people might post. You want as many people posting as possible, which means you have to set up your page to allow anyone to post.

It is also possible to buy advertising on Facebook. This involves a mysterious process where Facebook tracks users' conversations and preferences in order to feed them what they consider to be appropriate ads. You pay when someone clicks on your practice ad. The jury is still out as to whether anyone is benefiting from this, but things change fast with social media, and I think it will soon reach a point where it is cost-effective, so it would be worth experimenting with and getting ahead of the crowd.

The following additional sites are listed in order of how I see their importance in growing and promoting your practice.

Google+: This is the new big entry into social media, and Google's attempt to compete with Facebook. It is a very well thought out service, and they worked very hard to make it better than Facebook in many ways. Almost 200 million people have signed up for it as of this printing, and with the strong growth of Android® phones there will be a lot more action on it. Google+ allows you to easily put people in different "circles" so you can control who sees your individual posts. They also have video hangouts, which are like video conference calls, and free telephone calls. You certainly need to put your business here, and I recommend you follow the same procedures as you do with your Facebook page, even though right now you shouldn't expect to see any real activity. People are signing up on Google+ and then just going back to using Facebook every day (where all their friends already are).

Google has also implemented a brilliant combination of their search function and your Google+ information and posts, and are calling it Google "Search Plus Your World." What they are doing is analyzing the information from people's posts on Google+ and the people within their circles to make the results more personally targeted. So instead of simply providing a search result that anyone else would get, Google is going to factor in postings that your friends may have put up on their Google+ page, as well as gauge your own preferences based on your own posts. And it will offer all those results to you, which may include comments or recommendations made by your friends, even photos and videos they posted if Google thinks they are relevant to your search. I think it's a game changer for the search world, and maybe for social media. So I highly recommend you get involved.

After you build your Google+ business page, remember that you can't do promotions directly on your page. You can only post a different Web address where there is an offer. Facebook allows promotions on your page, but it's restricted to their apps (even though you see people violating this all the time).

Of course, this doesn't mean you'll get any real traffic to your Google+ page. Right now most people are using Google+ for technology-focused business pages. As I said, I do believe behavior will expand beyond that. What will matter most is that *Google* sees your page and will include it in "Search Plus Your World" searches if your patients have added you to one of their circles. You will come up in more searches, more often, with more detail. And I can't stress this point enough: Remember the Google matrix: YouTube®, Blogger, Google+, Google Places, Google reviews and Android. These Google properties are all getting blended together by this monster search engine. Much of your online search strategy relates to this matrix. Add to this the fact that Google now owns Motorola®, which will accelerate the use of Android on smart phones. The more comprehensive your approach, the more these elements will all reinforce each other and increase your online relevance. As I mentioned, no one knows all the elements and data Google factors into a search result, but you'd have to be a fool not to imagine that their own properties figure heavily into it.

YouTube: Video is king right now in the search world. Not only that, don't forget that YouTube is also owned by Google. This means they believe that video content is valuable, relevant information and therefore needs to be constantly cataloged by their search engine and incorporated into their search result assessments. What's more, videos are very effective and people tend to watch them even more than they read content on websites—significantly more, if you believe the statistics. YouTube videos currently get *3 billion viewings a day.*

You need to make it a habit to generate short videos on a regular basis. They are not only useful on YouTube, but also for your website, your Facebook and Google+ pages, your Places sites, your blogs and even on Twitter. These videos do not have to be brilliant or well-shot. They can be done with a smart phone or an iPad, or there are excellent HD video cameras for a few hundred dollars.

So what do you make videos of? Initially, start with a short video by the dentist, describing why you went into dentistry and what type of practice you have. Forty-five seconds is plenty. Do it over and over until you like it. The script should go something like this:

> "I'm Doctor Jackson, and I wanted to introduce you to my practice. I became a dentist because I wanted a profession where I could make a big difference in people's lives. I believe we've created a practice that you'll find comfortable and friendly, and we use all the latest technology to offer you the best, fastest, most comfort-conscious dentistry possible. I invite you to come in and meet our team and see for yourself, and I look forward to meeting you myself and taking great care of you."

Then you can also do a quick video tour of your office, and after that, occasional interviews with patients, some descriptions of treatments you offer, and whatever else you feel the urge to record. Post it on YouTube, as well as all the other places I mentioned.

Perhaps the most powerful videos you can make are patient testimonials. If a consumer sees a written testimonial on your website, for example, he gives it almost no credence because he assumes it was written by your spouse or your best friend. Video testimonials, on the other hand, are extremely credible. And surprisingly easy to do.

First, don't worry about them being a well-shot and edited video. I'm talking about using a smart phone and asking the patient to do a quick testimonial. The fact that it is not a polished video just increases its credibility. I would ask the patient, "Would you be willing to do a quick video testimonial for us?" (Obviously you'd ask a happy patient.) They may hesitate, but just say, "If you don't like it we won't use it. But just say your name and what it's like to be a patient of ours."

You will be amazed at what people will say speaking from the heart. They will give you 45 seconds of pure marketing magic. I've seen it happen countless times. And now you've got something for Facebook, your website, YouTube and wherever else you can put it. Do one a week and that's FIFTY a year! That's a tremendous amount of valuable content.

When it comes to YouTube, the most important part is your description of the video when you post it. Make sure the "tags" contain keywords like "dentistry," "teeth" and whatever you're describing in the video, as well as your name and your practice name. Posting everywhere not only offers a big advantage from an organic search standpoint, but it also gives your patients and potential patients that extra reassurance about your capability (as well as your general willingness to stay current with technology). And then it doesn't hurt to have your friends watch the videos on YouTube and rate them.

The next important step is to create your own YouTube "channel," which is essentially a location within YouTube where all your videos can be easily found. It's easy, and you would use the same gmail login that you use for your Google Places/ Google+ account. They will all become linked together.

Don't be afraid to make fun, playful videos. One dentist made a video of himself cleaning his dog's teeth. It was hugely popular. I know another dentist who decided to take the whole team out shoe shopping as a reward for a big month. That made a great video that really personalized the practice, and showed the spirit of fun they have.

Editing video has also become very easy, and if you can't do it, you probably know a teenager who could do it effortlessly in minutes. Again, these videos don't have to be Oscar®-level quality. Most, in fact, should be one continuous take. You also don't want them to be too big a file, because then they will upload slowly on your website. Make sure you control the size (megabytes) of the video depending on where you are putting it. I don't mean the length of the video (*which should always be under 90 seconds*) but the size of the digital file itself, and the resolution of the video. It doesn't need to be high resolution if someone is watching it in a small window on your website or on their phone. Remember, the last thing you want is a video that keeps pausing to upload because it's too big. People will stop watching 90 percent of the time if that happens.

Many dentists think this is an utter waste of time. They will ask me, "Who would read (or watch) all this stuff?" The answer, in part, is potential patients. But the big answer, as I mentioned, is the search engines. Google's raison d'être is to scan every scrap of information on the Internet and serve up the best results to the people who make search requests. And that ultimately means that your practice name will come up more often in a natural search. The sooner you do these things, the more ahead of the pack you will be. And that will take on greater significance as the field gets more and more crowded.

Blogs: Dentists ask me, "Who the heck would read my blog?" "No one," I reply, "Except Google. And that's why you do it."

You need to write a blog and post regularly. Use WordPress®or Blogger® to set up a theme format. They are both very user-friendly and the basic plan is free. Blogger also happens to be owned by Google. (I have a deep-seated suspicion that this means all the material on Blogger comes up sooner in a search. I could just be paranoid.) Try to do a blog entry at least every week, or have one of your team members do it. Make it personal, interesting, fairly brief and relevant to your practice and to dentistry in general.

When writing a blog, it's important to write in short paragraphs—usually only a sentence or two. Add a photo whenever possible, and even video. It's not that hard anymore, and the quality is not that critical. Also, be sure to "tag" and "categorize" your blog with all the relevant content. This makes your article more searchable (which, don't forget, is why you are doing it). You should not expect a whole group of people to be fascinated by your blog every week. There are more than 20 million blogs at this point. What you are striving for is to have relevant content in as many forms as possible. A blog helps. And ideally, you then post your blog onto your website (or, if you have a dynamic website, it can be set to post automatically).

Twitter®: While this may seem the ultimate frivolity or time waster (either unnecessary or bizarrely narcissistic), it is a powerful medium at this point. It works like this: You make very short entries (140 characters or less) on a regular basis, and at the same time try to accumulate followers, like your patients and friends. If you have a blog, you should mention it on Twitter each time you post a new entry. It doesn't take that much time (unless you start reading other people's posts, and then you can get sucked in for hours!) and it will all add up to something someday. You can also link photos and video to a tweet.

If you tweet on a regular basis, particularly about dentistry, it will show up on a Google search, as well as other search engines, which is perhaps the best reason to be putting something out there. It will affect the ranking of your website— and you want to do as much as possible to reinforce that from several directions.

Some practices are also using Twitter to post openings in their schedule, or promotional posts like discount whitening for people who come in the next week. Obviously you need your patients following you on Twitter for them to see this, but the advantage is that people can "retweet" any post you do, so it spreads virally (sometimes, if people care). You can do something similar by e-blasting your patients, but Twitter often has a greater tendency to spread. Not everyone is reading everything on their Twitter site, but a lot of people look all day long. Strange, I know, but it's a new world.

LinkedIn: I believe it is valuable to have a LinkedIn page, which should only take you an hour or so to set up, but I don't see that it is necessary to post a lot or aggressively pursue connections at this time. Simply update it when you have a new blog entry. It is searchable, so it is worth the time to go through all the steps to make your profile comprehensive. Look at it as one more piece in the puzzle. And you can make it so that one post shows up everywhere: Twitter, Facebook and LinkedIn. Use Tweetdeck or Hootsuite and you can do this easily.

Pinterest®: This site has really come into heavy usage in just three years, but it has very specific audience behavior. It is essentially a digital scrapbook, where the user posts images that they like from various websites, which of course link back to those sites. Though I've been told that dentists can get some value out of it, right now I don't see that people would search Pinterest for a dentist and come up with satisfying results. And to me that's the name of the game.

The site activity is primarily centered around food, fashion and do-it-yourself items. This may change and evolve over time, but I wouldn't get distracted by it at this time. Right now it just looks like a glorified Yellow Pages when you search for dentists in a particular area.

Instagram®: This is really just an easy way to create photos and short videos, enhance them in all sorts of interesting ways, and then share them. This company was bought by Facebook, so it really is a part of that service, but by itself it is only a good way to create the imagery that you would use elsewhere. You would have to generate a list of followers, which is time much better spent getting Facebook likes.

FourSquare®: This is a "check-in" and review environment for businesses, particularly restaurants, and I don't see it catching on at all with dentists. Facebook is starting to dominate the "check-in" space, so this company struggles with trying to be a giant-killer. If this becomes a viable medium for dental practices I'll eat my phone.

Everything beyond Facebook, Google+ and YouTube, I consider much less significant, and should occupy much less of your time. But you could probably make any one of these work well if you narrow-focused your attention to it. The fact is, each site has its own group of loyal followers. I prefer bigger targets, but you can try what appeals to you.

YELP, GOOGLE AND THE NEW WORLD OF ONLINE REVIEWS

The biggest trend in online search behavior is consumer reviews. People love online reviews, and once they start reading reviews, they want them for everything. They read book reviews on Amazon before they buy a book. They won't travel without going to www.tripadvisor.com. They won't see a movie without checking on Rotten Tomatoes. They want restaurant reviews, hotel reviews, and in general don't buy anything unless they can read reviews about it first. Fifty-seven percent of consumers say they trust reviews as a research source.[19] And if they can't find a review about a specific product or business, they move on to one that does have reviews. We all like to solicit opinions before we make a buying decision, and the Internet makes this exponentially easier. And more and more, this is how they will choose a dentist. This shift will affect your website, your social media strategy and even your practice policies.

There are many websites that show or gather reviews, but perhaps the most well-known site that is purely reviews is Yelp. Also, as part of its own expanding search service, Google now gathers reviews for businesses and will list them as part of a search result. There are dozens of sites that show reviews for dentists, Angie's List®, HealthGrades® and Dr. Oogle® being the next most popular. Our 1-800-DENTIST website also shows patient reviews for our members.

If you don't know what Yelp is, it's a website where people can review any business they want (and they don't need the business owner's permission to do it). They merely find the business listed on Yelp.com—and Yelp has almost every business in their database—and post whatever they want to write about that business, and then give it a rating from one to five stars. Even if you've never heard of Yelp, or never gone onto the website, it is very likely that you and your practice have been reviewed there. Currently more than 70 percent of practices have at least one review.

And this is very important to remember: You have no ability to remove a Yelp review if someone posts one about your business. People have tried. A dentist recently spent the past two years suing both Yelp and the patient who had posted a negative review about her practice. The court finally ruled that she needed to pay $80,000 in legal costs to the patient and dismissed the case. This is the rule: Reviews are considered free speech, protected by the First Amendment. So, unless it's profane or completely provable libel, you can't get it removed.

Anyone can go onto Yelp and search for a business and Yelp will provide search results based on the star rating of the business by reviewers, as well as the most recent reviews. Angie's List and Dr. Oogle are similar review sites, though Angie's List requires you to become a subscriber in order to search or post reviews. Dr. Oogle and HealthGrades are for all medical categories. All of them are growing in usage, but Google and Yelp get much more traffic.

People put a lot of stock in online reviews. In fact, we have people who call 1-800-DENTIST and, after we recommend a specific practice, they'll go online and look up the dentist on Yelp while still on the phone with us. Then they tell us what star rating the dentist has. Fortunately, we already know this rating, but most dentists don't have a clue the level to which this is happening.

Yelp has a tendency to "filter" positive reviews, especially if they are posted by someone who doesn't do a lot of Yelp reviews. This can be frustrating, as the negative reviews will all appear automatically. And if someone searches your name, if you are not a paying advertiser on Yelp, then when your result comes up the consumer is also going to see ads for thirteen, yes, *thirteen* other dentists. The only way I know to keep positive reviews from getting filtered, short of paying to advertise on Yelp (which miraculously releases the reviews from the filter, I've noticed), is to find a patient who is a regular Yelp reviewer—someone who has done more than 25 reviews for various businesses—and ask them to write a review. That review almost always stays unfiltered.

What you want to keep in mind is that Google is certainly indexing its own reviews, but it is also indexing Yelp's and all the others, so this will affect your SEO. The rumor is that

Google is planning to start evaluating the language of the review and giving it a score that will also affect your relevance. Stuff changes fast online.

In the digital age, you need an active process for generating a steady stream of positive reviews. The best way to do this is by emailing your patients and asking them to do it for you. If you use a digital communication application like PatientActivator, then you can do an email campaign specifically asking patients to go to your Yelp or Google page and post a review.

You don't need new reviews every day. A couple a week is great. The important element is for them to be recent. The older they are, the more reluctant people are to give them credibility.

"PLACES" ON GOOGLE, YELP AND FACEBOOK

Each of these websites has sections of their database for consumers that are location-specific, and all have an application for smart phones. On Google, it will be in their maps, which now also appear as part of general search results for businesses. On Yelp, it will be in their individual listing of your business, and on Facebook it is primarily when someone uses the mobile application and "checks in." With each of these locations, you want to put as much accurate information as possible about your business.

Google is important for two reasons: They are the undisputed kings of search, particularly in the mapping arena, and they also let you add a significant amount of information about your business. To add this information you need to claim your business by going to www.google.com/places and searching for your practice. You will see a link somewhere on the page that will say, "Claim your business listing on Google" or words to that effect. Sign up, or sign in if you have a gmail address already, and then claim your business, which involves them calling your business phone number and giving you a code to log in and claim it.

Once you have done this, you can now add a load of information. Make sure all the information about your phone numbers and address is accurate. Add photos of the dentist and the practice. Put in your office hours. Put in all the dental services you offer. You can even add a few videos, like your practice tour and testimonials. And you can put special offers such as first time visit discounts. And lastly, this is where you will see the reviews of your business that people have done on Google, and where you will send your patients to review your practice. As I mentioned, this will also link to your YouTube channel.

Also, on Google there may be multiple listings for your business. You will need to claim them all individually and close all but one, otherwise you don't know which one people will see.

Yelp is slightly different, although the process is the same. Go to biz.yelp.com. Click the big button that says "Create your free account now." On the next page you will search for your business, claim it with the same process of them sending you a code, and then once again you can add all sorts of data about your business. This will also allow you to respond to reviews about your practice on Yelp.

This is free advertising and free SEO combined. Do this immediately if you haven't already.

Facebook doesn't technically have a "places" function, but people can check-in to your practice even if you haven't set up your page yet. This is because Facebook has most businesses already listed in a directory. Once you start your page, when you put in your address Facebook will try to link your previous check-ins. This is valuable because now when patients come to your office they can "check in" on Facebook on their smart phones, and their friends will see that they are at your practice. Social media doing its job!

MONITORING YOUR REPUTATION AND DEALING WITH NEGATIVE REVIEWS

Now that you've claimed your business on these sites, you need to be continually tracking to see if there are negative postings about your practice. Monitoring your online reputation needs to be an ongoing process.

I'm going to explain how to approach a negative online review from a patient, but first understand that when most people read reviews, they look at them like Olympic skating scores. In other words, they disregard the best one and the worst one and give much more credence to the reviews in the middle. They know that the glowing, wonderful review in perfect English was written by your spouse or your office manager, and that the nasty, negative review was from some misguided, cranky person who hates you. At this point in life, if we have any success, we all have some nut who hates us. In fact, if consumers don't see a negative review, they may assume that you wrote all the reviews yourself and give no credence to any of them. So don't sweat one or two negative reviews. The goal is to have so many positive reviews from your good patients that it overwhelms any negativity.

If you see a negative review this is what you do:

STEP ONE: CONTACT THE PATIENT.

Email the patient directly and ask him if you can remedy the situation. You can do this as the business owner, now that you've claimed your business, even though the reviewer is anonymous. Let the patient know that you're sorry that he is displeased and if there's anything you can do, you're glad to do it. If he tells you that you can do something, by all means do it, and then ask him to please take the negative review down. (Don't ask him to do that first. Fix the problem first.)

STEP TWO: RESPOND TO THE REVIEW.

If you can't get the patient to take the review down and fix the situation yourself, now you need to respond to the negative review. And there are two things to remember here:

1. Always respond to negative reviews, but don't be defensive. Ever.
2. Use the response to essentially write an ad for your practice.

For example, the most common bad review is a patient saying that the dentist told them they needed a lot of dental work and wanted this huge amount of money—then they went to another dentist who told them that they only needed $400 of dentistry. So they think the first dentist is a crook and love the second dentist (when in reality, the first dentist presented too soon and the second dentist is afraid to present any comprehensive dentistry).

So how do you respond? The urge is to go on the defensive and insist that the patient misunderstood, the other dentist is a hack, etc. This makes you look bad and at best, accomplishes nothing. At worst, it exacerbates the situation to a war of words. Instead, respond by essentially writing an ad for your practice. Write something like this:

> "We're sorry that this patient felt that way about their visit. At our practice we offer a very high standard of care and sometimes this may seem expensive at first, but we believe taking care of your teeth is very important to your general well-being and your overall health—and so we try to fully inform our patients as to their needs. We do hope this patient finds a dental practice that they love and go to regularly, because that is what's most important."

See what this does? It takes a negative situation and gives you an opportunity to say that you offer high-quality dentistry and it's too bad this person didn't want it. This makes you seem like the calm, sane person, and attracts the right patients to your practice.

STEP THREE: LET IT DIE.

Once you've responded, don't get into it anymore. If they respond back, leave it alone. You never win the war of words online.

STEP FOUR: INVITE YOUR PATIENTS TO RESPOND.

Whenever there is a negative review, the best response comes from your patients. Ask your best patients if they'd be willing to comment on the negative review, and you'll be amazed at how they will rally to your cause. And there is nothing more powerful than seeing a list of responses from patients contradicting a negative review. Viewers will see that and be extremely impressed that your own patients will rally to your defense.

A friend of mine was so embarrassed about a negative review on Yelp that he didn't want his patients to see it. I told him, "Your best patients would be outraged to know someone was saying this about you. They will go online and rip this person to shreds. Just let them know about it, and watch what happens." Sure enough, a week later the person took the negative review down because my friend's patients pretty much humiliated the reviewer. You have patients who love you who will come to your defense, and they can say whatever they want and it doesn't put you in the middle of it.

As the business owner, you are allowed to respond to a review on Yelp and on Google. On Angie's list, people can only review you if they are a subscriber. And you can only respond if you are a subscriber, which is not that expensive, and I think worthwhile.

There is a new trend going on where patients are threatening practices with bad reviews. I know dentists who have patients who owe them money but are refusing to pay, saying they'll post negative reviews everywhere if the dentist sends them to collections. Don't allow yourself to be held hostage. One or two bad reviews, as I said, is not the end of the world. But let's not forget, this is extortion. And if they were dumb enough to say something like that on your voicemail, then prosecute.

I hope you can see that this is why you need to continuously monitor your online reputation. You need to know the day something negative goes up about you. There are various ways to do this. You can set up a Google Alert, which will send you an email every time your name is mentioned in some public document, but that's pretty limited. You need to make it someone's job to go onto the main review sites—ideally daily—and see if anything new has been posted about your practice.

The best way is a tool we created called ReputationMonitor (see Appendix I). It searches the entire Web for every mention of your practice, and brings the results into a single dashboard that you can look at and decide what you need to deal with. It shows all the possible directory sites where you are listed, and there can be dozens of them, and all the online reviews and social media comments. It will also send an email or text alert any time that a review has been posted about your practice. This vastly simplifies the daily monitoring that you should be doing.

Also, if you are using a digital communication application like PatientActivator, then one of its functions is to email each patient three days after their visit and ask for a review. This not only gives you valuable feedback, and a review to post on social media and your website, but it preempts the unhappy patient from going on Yelp or Google, and writing something that you have no control over. Feedback is always worthwhile, but you want to be able to control its distribution whenever possible.

THE FAST WAY TO GET FACEBOOK POSTS AND YELP REVIEWS:

Here is a great technique for getting people to post on your Facebook and Google+ pages, and also to get Yelp reviews. Buy one or two iPads (the cheapest ones, since you will only need the WiFi function and very little storage). Then, when a patient is in the waiting room or logging idle time in the operatory, you can ask them if they would like to go on Facebook and post on your fan page. They can even take a picture or record a video with the iPad, and can post those.

Ask if they use Yelp and if they would be willing to review your practice. Most people won't mind doing it, especially if you also include a few games like Angry Birds™ on the iPads.

I recommend you go to www.skinit.com, where you can buy adhesive covers and frames for your iPads, and custom design them with your Facebook username right on the front—plus the URL of your Yelp location. By the way, DO NOT ask them to do a Google review on the iPad, or on any device that is using your office WiFi. Google will disregard multiple reviews that come from the same device. That's why emailing your patients is the best way to request Google reviews.

So many people use Facebook on their smart phones that they could do it on their own device just as easily. But the tablet makes it a little more appealing, in my mind.

As I previously mentioned, it is also essential to get a release from all your patients to use photography and video of them. If they won't sign one, don't use their image in any way. (They, of course, can still post any image of themselves without this.) This goes for staff members as well. Employees should all sign such a release upon being hired. You want full rights to use the imagery on your websites, on YouTube and all social media and search engines. And you don't want to have to take anything down because you didn't get a release and they don't want to let you use it anymore. The release should include language to this effect:

> "I [person's name] give my permission to [practice name] to use my image or be recorded in still or video photography or any other medium, for use in all media including social media, in perpetuity throughout the universe, for any purpose whatsoever." Have them sign and date it.

This is a must-do. You can get a release form from www.legalzoom.com, or use a local attorney to make sure it is appropriate for your state.

Lastly, remember that you can pay to advertise on Yelp, Angie's List, and of course on Google. What you're really paying for is for your practice to come up at the top of the search. It will be highlighted, and will show whatever reviews you have, good or bad. You can only pay to advertise on Angie's List if you have a high enough rating. They are the only ones who restrict in this way. You can advertise on Facebook, as I mentioned earlier, and small ads will appear on the right side of the user's screen. You will pay every time someone clicks on the ad. You can control a lot of the parameters with Facebook, and have it only appear to females over 30, for example, as well as limit it to your neighborhood. This is essentially part of your online ad budget, which includes buying keywords.

OTHER IMPORTANT ONLINE STEPS:

1) Claim your name everywhere online before someone else does. Of course, this starts with the URLs, or domain names, for yourself and your practice. Use your middle initial or full name if you have to. It might cost you $40 to register the URL at GoDaddy.com®, but better for you to have it than anyone else. And buy it for 10 years. It helps with search engine optimization that you own it long-term. Along with ".com," you should also claim your practice name in the ".net" and ".org" versions. You can redirect any domain name to any other domain name, so don't worry about having too many—they can all ultimately take users to the same website. You may also want to consider registering misspellings of your name.

Also make sure you claim your Vanity URL, or username, for your Facebook fan page This is recognized in an online search, so you want to have your practice name if possible. Eventually most names won't be available, so the sooner you do this the better. It doesn't have to be your whole practice name, and often that's not available anyway. It can be a shortened version of it, because you are looking to put it on business cards, or make it easy for someone to type in on an iPhone or iPad. In other words, your practice name could be Fred Joyal's Magnificent Smiles of Brentwood. A username like www.facebook.com/magsmiles would be fine. You're striving for ease of typing and no misspellings.

Grab your name on LinkedIn, Twitter and as many other places as you can. Get a gmail email address, even if you don't plan on using it right now. It will serve as a log in for YouTube, Google+ and more.

2) Comment on other blogs. Take some time to read various health blogs, and don't be afraid to add your own thoughts. (Then refer to something in your own website or blog, and link back to it.)

3) Get organizations you belong to or boards that you sit on to add your bio to their website. Have you donated mouthguards to the local elementary school's soccer team? Make sure they acknowledge you in their online newsletter—that will likely come up in a search too. And be sure you're listed with your local chamber of commerce or Better Business Bureau. That way anyone looking you up online will see how involved you are in the community and the positive impact you are having. You never know when an existing or new patient will go digging, so the more entities you have out there vouching for you, the better.

ONLINE APPOINTMENTS

I understand that dentists are very protective of their appointment "book." But the wave of the future is that people are going to expect to be able to log in to your practice as a patient to make and change their appointments online 24 hours a day. As terrifying as this sounds, there are password protections and rules you can put in place that will keep people from totally messing up your schedule. There are group practices that are already doing this successfully with tens of thousands of patients. I'm saying it's coming, so mentally prepare yourself. Most likely your practice management software will have this capability in the next year or two, and you should start to incorporate it into your website.

ACTION ITEMS:

Basically, everything in this chapter is an action item. I would approach them in this order:

1. Get a good, dynamic website where you can add content like testimonials and reviews, your blog, and videos.

2. Update all your information on the Places: Google, Yelp and Facebook.

3. Start a Facebook business fan page and a Google+ page.

4. Assign someone to post and comment on social media and to monitor your online reputation.

5. Claim your name everywhere.

6. Start an ongoing system of generating online reviews from patients.

7. Become an amateur videographer.

8. Everything else.

CHAPTER 24

FINAL
THOUGHTS

Let me first say that I may be wrong about some of these things, and it's possible that not every concept in this book will hold true for your practice or neighborhood. Advertising is, after all, a game of probabilities—one that is evolving faster than ever. That being said, I ask that you don't discard those approaches that may be useful for you because I may have occasionally missed the mark when it comes to your own individual situation.

Many people may read this book and think that I'm just talking about how to get rich. That's not my point (although, hopefully, it's a byproduct). My goal has been to get you to believe in yourself—and to get you fired up about what a great profession dentistry is and how happy a life you and your whole team can have practicing it. I wrote this book to attack the old mindset. In 10 years, I want people to hold dentists in the highest esteem, grateful for what dentistry has done for the quality of their lives.

Sure, making money is great, but over the years I've seen too many people who are cash-wealthy and satisfaction-poor. True happiness and deep satisfaction come from how you live your life and the impact you have on others.

I'm not much of a sports fan, but I will tell you my favorite sports story. It's not about an inspiring victory—but rather a most inspiring loss. It happened at a final conference game of a women's college softball league in 2005. With two runners on base and one strike against her, Sara Tucholsky did something she had never done before—hit the ball for a home run straight over the center field fence. But the glory was brief. She missed first base, and as she turned back to tag the base, she collapsed with a knee injury. She crawled back to first base, but could go no farther.

Here was the dilemma (and this is really the beauty of baseball, that arcane rules so often affect the outcome): In order for all three runs to count, she had to run all the bases *herself.* If she used a designated runner, her home run would become a single, giving up the very runs that would put her team, Western Oregon University, in the lead.

So what did Central Washington, the opposing team, do? By general agreement, two of their players scooped Sara up and *carried her around the bases.* The first baseman from Central Washington later said, "In the end, it wasn't about winning or losing so much. It was about this girl. She hit it over the fence and was in pain, and she deserved a home run."

They could have easily insisted that she use a designated runner, and their team most likely would have won the game. But they chose to risk losing by doing what I consider to be the height of sportsmanship. They did lose—and didn't advance to the playoffs as a result—but if my daughter had been on that losing team, I would have been exploding with pride.

This is the lesson in it for me: In the end, it isn't about how much you made; it's how you played. I see this as the core of true happiness for people in any profession. If you dedicate yourself to taking care of people, to seeing how many lives you can improve, then I assure you that you will have made more than enough money.

"In the end, it isn't about how much you made; it's how you played."

One last thought: Don't beat yourself up about everything in this book that you're not yet doing. There's a Chinese proverb that says, "The best time to plant a tree was 20 years ago; the second best time is today." Get started, but don't take everything on at once because you most likely won't complete any of it. The fact is, doing any one or two of these things, making them part of the fabric of your practice, will yield significant results. Pick one, work on it, then go back and pick another one or two to add to the mix. But commit to doing something tomorrow. One thing. And watch what happens.

Most of all, be proud of what you do. You can have a great life and change many lives along the way.

ACKNOWLEDGMENTS

I always get irritated when the winner at an awards ceremony gets up and reads a list of all the people they want to thank. And now I'm about to do the same thing. I'll try not to make it boring.

First, I want to thank Dr. John Chaves, a good friend who ten years ago encouraged me to start speaking at dental seminars. Without that time at the podium all this material would not have materialized.

Two men were responsible for me getting my start in advertising: Peter Stranger and Ken Berris. Although our paths don't cross as often as I'd like, I'll never forget their guidance and generosity of spirit, and am eternally grateful for lighting the spark in me to find my true calling.

I want to thank Dr. Paul Homoly in general, but especially for his speaker training. It has proven invaluable, and much of his exceptional knowledge about case presentation and communication has appeared in this book as well. Also, many thanks to his team, Joan Cianciolo and Janet Plantier, who assiduously proofread and critiqued the first draft, comma by comma.

Thanks to the wonderful Linda Miles for her terrific comments and corrections, and her general inspiration. She exemplifies the philosophy of abundance with her generosity to me and the entire dental industry.

To Dr. Louis Malcmacher, whose insights are always razor-sharp. I hope to be half the speaker he is someday.

To Dr. Howard Farran, who believes in me more than I do myself, and whose insights into the business of dentistry are always a mega-dose of reality.

To Dr. Tim Driscoll, for his deeply moving story of one of his patients. I seldom tell it without tearing up.

Thanks to Dr. Bill Dorfman, for his friendship and for showing me to what great heights a dentist can truly ascend if he puts his mind to it.

Thanks to Drs. John and Cathy Jameson, who teach and inspire me and my whole team. And for that unforgettable weekend out on the ranch.

And a special thanks to my friend Imtiaz Manji, who inspires me with his wisdom and awes me with his knowledge. He taught me volumes about leadership and successful business practices, and to be unconditional in my commitments—and in return I taught him to love sushi.

To the many industry leaders who give me podium time: Rich and Dave Madow of TBSE fame, Heather Colicchio with AADOM, Drs. Sameer Puri and Tarun Agarwal of the Townie Meeting, and Gary Takacs. A special thanks to Dr. Mark Morin and his outrageous team at the Great Lakes Education Center for the most exotic speaking locations anyone could ask for.

I would also like to thank the industry publishers and editors whose continued friendship, receptivity and openness to my ideas and articles have inspired me to keep coming up with new ones to put down on paper: Lyle Hoyt, Dr. Joe Blaes and the team at PennWell/*Dental Economics*™, Kevin Henry at Advanstar Communications, Dr. Tom Giacobbi at *Dentaltown*, Dan Perkins and Tony Angelini at *Inside Dentistry*®, and John Schwartz and Dr. Jeff Rohde at Dentalcompare.

To Paul Guggenheim, president of Patterson Dental Supply, Inc., who is always a calm and enlightening presence, and an inspiration to me as a leader.

A special thanks to Michael Augins for letting me deep inside the workings of the CEREC business, and for being a good friend and faithful supporter of this book.

I'm grateful to all my partners and team members at Futuredontics, who both generate this knowledge that I'm passing on and gave much-needed comments and advice on the initial draft of the book.

No one can successfully edit his own book, and I'm no exception. Thanks to David Dee, Sarah Swidron and especially Brian Becker, who all toiled at breakneck speed to decipher and incorporate 20 people's input and pound the manuscript into shape. And to Jill Teeples and Zoe Korstvedt, who brought clarity to my scribbled graphics.

Also, I want to thank Arthur Gu and Kim Fuller, who executed the recording of this book for the audio version with patience and painstaking diligence. They didn't yawn once.

A very special thanks goes out to Tony Hsieh, the CEO of Zappos.com®, for his extreme generosity to my whole team, and for inspiring our core values. I highly recommend visiting their facility in Las Vegas to experience the ultimate in corporate culture and observe a near-perfect execution of infusing marketing into every aspect of a business.

I must express my extreme appreciation to all the 1-800-DENTIST members for the privilege of serving all of you these many years, and for all the wonderful feedback and insights you give me into what day-to-day dentistry is about.

Lastly, I want to thank two partners. First, my original business partner, Gary Saint Denis, without whom I would have never gotten into this business, and to whom I am eternally grateful for the steadfast and true partner he has always been. And second, to my life partner Mira, the joyful, shining love of my life. She allowed me to write for hours a day while we were on vacation without ever complaining, and made sure I was well-fed and highly entertained the rest of the time.

FUTUREDONTICS'
SERVICES

OUR PURPOSE

You are most likely familiar with the brand name, 1-800-DENTIST, but our corporate name is Futuredontics, Inc. and we have evolved beyond just attracting new patients for practices to an integrated suite of marketing products, all designed to make the promotion of your practice easier, and the communication with your patients more efficient and more effective.

The purpose of our business is fairly simple: We want you to treat more patients, more often. And every product we design is intended to fulfill that in some way. We also believe in a marriage of highly skilled humans with highly sophisticated technology. While many businesses are trying to automate everything, we believe in providing that personal aspect that can only be accomplished with real live people.

Dr. Gordon Christensen visited our headquarters in Los Angeles a few years ago, and after the tour he said, "I don't think dentists have any idea how hard you work for them." It's true. To the outside world, we run advertising, people call us or visit our website, find a dentist and the dentists pay us to be listed on the service. But there is a lot more to it. And now there are more services, as well.

We invite you to visit our office in Los Angeles and see this purpose in action. We think you'll see us the way Dr. Christensen did.

Here are the services we currently offer:

1-800-DENTIST REFERRAL SERVICE

The greatest misconception is that any dentist can join 1-800-DENTIST, simply by writing a check. That may be true for other advertising programs, but not ours. We have one of the most stringent screening processes in dentistry, for one simple reason: The integrity of the 1-800-DENTIST brand matters much more to us than the money any individual dentist could pay us.

We check to see if a dentist's license is in good standing. We get a history of peer review and malpractice from the state dental board or board of dental examiners, and ensure that the prospective member dentist has proper and current levels of malpractice insurance. The dentist also fills out a five-page profile that allows us to have more detailed and searchable information than any other dental referral service. And we get constant feedback on our dentists from the patients we send them, by emailing a survey to every caller or visitor to our website. And yes, we have kicked dentists off the program for failing to meet our requirements.

We do not attempt to do clinical assessments of dentists, because there is a great deal of subjectivity in that. I've found two unique phenomena among dentists. First, if you asked a room full of dentists who among them thought that they were in the top 10 percent clinically, 100 percent would raise their hands. Sorry, but it's not statistically possible for that to be true. Second, for every dentist, no matter how well-trained, or how great a reputation he has, there is someone out there who thinks he's a hack. Because of this, we have stayed away from clinical assessments and have stuck to the objective requirements of the state licensing entities.

The other myth is that somehow the only dentists who join 1-800-DENTIST are the dentists who are so bad that they can't get patients on their own. Let me say first that it is getting harder and harder to just get new patients on your own. But, more importantly, we have members whose clinical skills and chairside manner I would consider among the finest in the country. They generate tons of word of mouth from the patients we send them and the patient feedback we receive about our member dentists is overwhelmingly positive. I think that's a strong indicator of the quality of our membership in the patients' eyes.

Once dentists have met with our approval, they pay us monthly on a per-lead basis to be part of the service, or previously, a flat monthly fee for an average number of leads. Notice I said *leads*. We can get them to respond, but we can't get them all the way into the practice. That's the dentist's and the front desk's job. But we also provide tools to help with that. When you pay on a per-lead basis you can set the limit as to how many patient leads you would like on a monthly basis. We may not always reach that maximum, but we won't exceed it.

We operate a 24/7/365 call center. We also operate a website, which allows patients to search on their own for the dentist, but when the patient calls the phone number in the dentist's profile, it currently rings to our call center. This way, whether the potential patient has dialed us directly or has come through the website, our staff has the opportunity to pre-qualify and screen them to make sure that they go to the right office.

Whenever possible, we personally introduce the potential patient to the practice. We can see the office hours of the dentist, and call them with the potential patient on the line and then hand the lead over to the practice with an introduction. The main reason we do this is to increase the likelihood that the appointment coordinator will put on her happy face and convert the caller into a patient. And the latest innovation is for us to be able to book the patient directly into your schedule, without you having to even call the patient yourself.

There are no "territories" per se, because we want to give a good consumer experience by giving the caller choices. Also, we are using primarily broadcast media and the Internet, and this generates results that do not spread evenly over every ZIP code. We are continuing to spend more and more in advertising every month so that we can reach more consumers and serve more dentists.

We promote the phone number and website with national and local TV advertising, as well as radio, Yellow Pages, online keyword bidding and occasionally billboards and other print media.

We also offer a considerable amount of support to practices to help teams convert media-generated callers into patients. We have handled millions of incoming calls and helped thousands of dentists, and we have a really good sense of how to maximize conversion of leads into patients.

The advantages to 1-800-DENTIST are these:

Sustainability: You are going to get predictable results for your investment for as long as you participate. We have dentists who have been members for 20 years or more—that only happens when something works, and works consistently. Many of our members do no practice advertising besides 1-800-DENTIST.

Screening: The patients we direct to you are much more likely to become long-term patients. This is because a high percentage of the people who call us are not referred to a member dentist. These callers may just have questions, or restricted insurance plans, or no way to pay. What this means is when we send a potential patient to your office, they are more likely to become a true patient of record than any other form of advertising you can do, which basically sends every call to your front desk, or your voicemail.

Simplicity: You don't have to figure out how to create the advertising, or how much to spend and where to spend it. That's our job. And it's our full-time job.

Support: We will teach you how to maximize your results, and we will give your team as much training as you ask for.

All in all, it's a pretty dandy service, and I hope you consider it for your practice. As I mentioned, we welcome any dentist and team to visit our office personally to see what we do and how we do it. We think you'll be surprised, and probably learn something.

PATIENT ACTIVATOR

PatientActivator is a digital communication product that interfaces directly with your software, performing a wide variety of time-saving and practice-building functions. Digital technology and your practice management software make it possible for you to reduce your workload while increasing production. I've spoken with users of PatientActivator who've told me that it's reduced the front desk workload by 40 percent. This means 40 percent more time to focus on the people who do need a phone conversation.

PatientActivator can send appointment reminders by email or text message automatically. At this point, many patients are not interested in a phone call as an appointment reminder, and you'll find that text and email are highly efficient ways to confirm and remind your patients. (It's also one more reason why you should get email addresses and mobile phone numbers from everyone.) This is the wave of the future—catch it and you'll save a lot of front desk time. The program can also send automated birthday greetings, newsletters, recall reminders and a lot more to help keep your patients coming back.

You can also do automated appointment reminders by telephone through PatientActivator. While this may seem impersonal, what it does is give your front desk the time to focus on conversations with patients that do require personal attention. People are getting more used to this, and you'll find it saves a tremendous amount of busy work for your staff.

With PatientActivator you can also control how each individual patient receives messages. If a patient wants only email and not text, you can set it up that way and change it any time, and it can be different for each patient. And you get daily updates on who we communicated with and what the result was.

One of the other benefits is it automatically solicits patient reviews that you can use to upload to your own website—and we also automatically post them to a separate microsite for you. This will boost your SEO, as well as give you great feedback from your patients. We also have a Reviews Builder tool that makes it easy to invite patients to write reviews for your practice on Google, Yelp and other major sites. As you remember from the online reviews section of Chapter 23, a steady stream of new, positive reviews has become more and more important. PatientActivator makes this easy and automatic.

PatientActivator will also send automatic dormant patient reminders to patients who haven't been in the practice in over a year. This is a special message designed to bring these patients back into regular care, and you'll be amazed at how effective this simple communication can be to get people back in your office and on track with their oral hygiene.

There is also something unique to PatientActivator, which is its smart phone application. With it you can see your schedule, your patient reviews, and a list of the patients you saw that day, so that you can make your evening check-in calls with the touch of a button. Most dentists like this feature the most.

Best of all, at least from a marketing standpoint, you can do marketing campaigns to your patients whenever you want. There are all sorts of messages that you can select and send to your patients by email or text, whether it's a Valentine's Day whitening special, a reminder to use up their insurance coverage before the end of the year, or a link to a video explaining the benefits of your CEREC, laser or other new technology—with a few keystrokes you can send them to your entire email list.

These tools fill your schedule, maximizing your production day, and they do it automatically. And they also tighten your recall, which is the name of the game in dentistry. More patients coming in more often means more production.

PatientActivator also has a number of social media features, such as a free Facebook app that lets people request an appointment directly from your Facebook fan page (you receive an immediate email request). It also has a module where you can easily promote special offers and coupons on your page.

There will be more and more features in this product as the digital world evolves, but right now is the time to start using a service like this and get your team used to the technology. They'll find that it saves them time, and the continual communication with your patients is going to increase your production. If you want to tighten your recall and boost your case acceptance with very little expense, this is the way to go.

Remember, you are trying to stay top-of-mind aware, and have all of your patients know everything the practice offers and why it's good for them. And the biggest challenge with internal marketing is to do it consistently month in and month out. PatientActivator makes that easy.

WEB DIRECTOR

We build dynamic websites that are both affordable and highly functional. Once built, you can add and change content yourself without having to call a webmaster. You can add photos, video, change text, almost anything.

Our websites adjust their format automatically for every device and browser, and use no Flash animation, and as browsers update we make the changes necessary to meet the new requirements or format, and you are not charged nor do you have to do an internal update.

Further, it includes a dedicated mobile website, which completely changes how your information is presented to give the best look and feel on a mobile device. And we use the same design elements to give you a consistent look on all your social media, and assist you in any setup you have not completed on all the social media sites.

The websites are built to load quickly and provide maximum SEO, so as your content changes you have the best chance of appearing on the first page in a search. We're honest, so we don't guarantee that, but we do everything technically possible to make that happen, and to make it easy for you to continually add the content that also improves your SEO.

There also is unlimited free customer service and support with WebDirector, and you are also not charged for any changes or updates.

REPUTATION MONITOR

This service searches the entire Internet for any mention of the dentist or the practice, and brings all the information onto a single screen where you can easily see what needs to be addressed. It looks at all directory sites (a task that would be almost impossible for a team member to accomplish on her own), all open online review sites, and all social media.

You can see places where information needs to be updated or corrected, and we simplify this process. You will also receive an alert anytime that a review is posted anywhere, as an email or a text, so that you can respond immediately.

REACTIVATION PRO

This service uses live operators, the same highly skilled personnel that we use in our 1-800-DENTIST call center, to call your dormant patients and attempt to reschedule them. We make these calls between 4 and 8pm, when we have a much greater likelihood of reaching those patients.

Our operators are focused completely on either bringing the patient back into the practice or determining why they are no longer interested. They do not have the interruptions that occur in a normal dental practice day, and therefore have a much higher success rate.

The value of the service is twofold: it brings dormant patients out of procrastination and into the office, and it also provides valuable feedback on why patients left. Often dentists value that feedback as much as they do the reactivated patients.

Each of these services is sold separately, but can be bundled together. And many of them complement each other and integrate features.

To find out more and for a demonstration on the products, visit www.futuredontics.com or call 1-866-903-9403.

SPEAKING ENGAGEMENTS

I also regularly speak about the topics covered in this book at tradeshows, study clubs, association meetings and private companies. I can tailor a presentation specifically for your audience, creating an experience that can be an interactive workshop or formal lecture covering the essentials of dental practice marketing, building the perfect team, fostering patient loyalty, etc. If you have a group of dental professionals interested in improving their practices through marketing, please contact my team at 1-800-222-5882.

MY BLOG: GO ASK FRED.COM

I post weekly on my blog, www.GoAskFred.com, as so much new information is emerging every month, particularly in the online world. It is also a great source of practical tips to improve team performance, enhance your practice marketing and learn what I'm learning every week meeting great dentists all over the country.

If you would like more copies of this book, they are available in hardcover or audio version at GoAskFred.com/freds-book/. There is also a Kindle version on Amazon, and a digital version on Nook and on iBooks. There are volume discounts available if you want copies for your whole team.

RECOMMENDED READING AND RESOURCES

BOOKS:

Dynamic Dentistry by Linda Miles

Powerful, practical advice from one of the masters. Her understanding of patients and the most effective ways to communicate with them are the foundation for a great practice. www.asklindamiles.com

Good to Great by Jim Collins

I've never met a business owner who couldn't benefit from this book. I consider it the best business book ever written.

Delivering Happiness: A Path to Profits, Passion and Purpose by Tony Hsieh, CEO, Zappos

I've learned more from Zappos than almost any other business. Tony is the businessman of the future. He is a master of corporate culture and customer service, and he's made a billion dollars doing it.

Switch: How to Change Things When Change is Hard by Chip and Dan Heath
> This is a phenomenal book, often counter-intuitive, on the most effective ways to bring about change in your life, your practice and your team.

Making It Easy for Patients to Say "Yes" by Dr. Paul Homoly, CSP
> In my experience, this is one of the best approaches out there to improve your case presentation—available as a book or audio program. www.paulhomoly.com

Great Communication = Great Success and *Collect What You Produce* by Dr. Cathy Jameson
> Both are cornerstone books on practice management. Not to be missed. www.jamesonmanagement.com

Customer Satisfaction Is Worthless by Jeffrey Gitomer
> This book covers the patient/customer loyalty concept in great detail.

Yes! 50 Scientifically Proven Ways to Be Persuasive by Noah J. Goldstein, Steve J. Martin and Robert B. Cialdini
> This marvelous short book shows you how people really think, and it's not the way you think they think.

WEBSITES AND SERVICES:

www.Dentaltown.com. This website is the ultimate destination for dentists exchanging information with each other. Pick a topic, and they've got pages and pages on it. And it's free to dental professionals.

www.takacslearningcenter.com. Gary Takacs has been a dental coach for more than 25 years. I know hundreds of practices who have transformed themselves while under his guidance. He also has a great blog and does excellent podcasts on all aspects of practice management.

www.TheDigitalDentist.com. Dr. Lorne Lavine hosts this website, which I consider the ultimate destination for dentists looking to understand the technological side of dentistry.

www.CERECdoctors.com. You'll find clinical videos here that will teach you how to handle almost any procedure that comes up. A fantastic tool for CEREC owners at every level, and you have unlimited access for a flat annual fee.

www.allfacebook.com. A terrific website that guides you through all the changes and mysterious and user-unfriendly aspects of Facebook.

www.logotournament.com and *www.crowdspring.com.* These websites are fantastic resources for crowdsourced design work. You put out your request, and what you want to pay, and depending on the price you offer, dozens of results will come back to you by designers from all over the world. Use them for logos, ads, Facebook pages, websites, stationery, whatever.

www.skinit.com. This is the website where you can get custom-designed, adhesive covers for your iPads or tablets, which will allow you to put your Facebook username and Yelp address right on the front.

HR for Health. This service provides an entirely digital solution for employee management, eliminating the considerable risks involved when proper legal procedures are not followed, from employee screening to reviews. The company is also a legal resource for the practice on anything related to the operation of your business to intricacies of protecting yourself from malpractice litigation. It also has a built in payroll/digital time-card function. www.hrforhealth.com

SEMINARS, CONSULTANTS & TRAINING:

Spear Education (formerly Scottsdale Center) is the new gold standard for clinical education. Interwoven with all the excellent training from instructors headed up by Dr. Frank Spear is the wisdom and experience of Imtiaz Manji, who has helped countless dentists reach amazing performance levels. They also have some of the best clinical courses to maximize your CEREC skills. www.speareducation.com

Fortune Management is a great resource for practice management from several angles, including team growth, practice systems and financial management. Headed up by Bernie Stoltz, an inspired speaker and leader, they will help you turn your practice into the success you've dreamed of. There are individual coaches for every region of the U.S. 1-800-628-1052 www.fortunemgmt.com

The Best Seminar Ever happens in Vegas every year, and it's a unique event. Put on by two dentists, Rich and Dave Madow, the event offers an environment of fun and learning that is not to be missed. The Madows also do smaller seminars around the country throughout the year, including detailed seminars on social media and how to capitalize on it, and they are all excellent. They also have several terrific DVDs on practice growth, and a number of very useful forms and highly effective sample letters for your practice. www.madow.com and www.tbse.com

American Association of Dental Office Managers is a great organization with an annual seminar, a magazine and continuing education that is valuable and rewarding and tailored especially for office managers. The network of members support each other all year round. Hard to beat. www.dentalmanagers.com

TGM Consulting with Lynette Conway is a front desk training program where the calls are recorded and the front desk team is coached to maximize effectiveness. I highly recommend this approach to improving call conversion, and Lynette has helped a lot of practices transform their front desk team. www.thegoldmeasure.com

Jameson Management Group has been around for a long time, with good reason. Their team of practice consultants offers some of the best coaching available, with an emphasis on effective marketing. www.jamesonmanagement.com

Banta Consulting is headed up by Lois Banta, who does general practice consulting in a very personal way, with a strong emphasis on telephone skills. www.bantaconsulting.com

Kimball Consulting has a very straightforward and time-tested approach to improving every aspect of your practice. Bill Kimball knows his stuff. www.kimballconsulting.com

Katherine Eitel does individual practice consulting and her greatest strength is scripting. She can skillfully guide your team with all the phrases that pay. www.katherineeitel.com

PRODUCTS:

CEREC. You don't have to read much of this book to know that I think CAD/CAM technology can transform your practice. In fact, I would say that it is the single most powerful technology for changing your practice from a parity service into a unique one. It will save you lab expenses, certainly, but it offers the great benefits of no second appointment and less discomfort because no temporaries are used. And that's a great marketing message. CEREC is sold in the U.S. exclusively through Patterson Dental, and gets better and more user-friendly with every version. You owe it to yourself to check it out. www.cerec.com

3-D Cone Beam technology, such as Sirona's Galileos. You can really amaze your patients by showing them three-dimensional imagery of the soft and hard tissue in their head. You can also place implants perfectly, and you can treat another major untapped category, sleep apnea. It is rapidly becoming the standard of care for implants.

FOOTNOTES

[1] ComScore Media Metrix Key Measures. February 1, 2013

[2] Center for Disease Control and Prevention. Oral Health for Older Americans, November 21, 2006. http://www.cdc.gov/OralHealth/publications/factsheets/adult_older.htm.

[3] Health Care Financial Administration. Online Dental Expenditure Data, 2002. http://www.cms.hhs.gov/statistics/nhe/default.asp.

[4] Berenson, Alex. Boom Time for Dentists, but Not for Teeth. New York Times, October 11, 2007. http://www.nytimes.com/2007/10/11/business/11decay.html?_r=2.

[5] Woolen, Mindy. Most Profitable Industries of 2008. Sageworks: Industry Trends, January 2009. http://www.sageworksinc.com/industrytrends/.

[6] Smith, Timothy A., Kroeger, Robert F., Lyon, H. Edward and Mullins, M. Raynor. Evaluating a Behavioral Method to Manage Dental Fear: A 2-year Study of Dental Practices. Journal of the American Dental Association, 1990.

[7] Albandar, J.M, Brunelle, J.A. and Kingman, A. Destructive Periodontal Disease in Adults 30 Years of Age and Older in the United States, 1988-1994. Journal of Periodontology, Vol. 70, No. 1, 1999.

8   First Research, Inc. Dentists Offices and Clinics, December 2008. http://www.mindbranch.com/Dentists-Offices-Clinics-R3470-2072/.

9   Zaltman, Gerald. Understanding Consumers' Thoughts & Feelings About Going to the Dentist: A ZMET Report to Futuredontics. Harvard University, September 1998.

10   Soussignan, R. Duchenne. Smile, Emotional Experience, and Automatic Reactivity: A Test of the Facial Feedback Hypothesis. Emotion, 2002. *2*(1), 52-74.

11   A Costly Dental Destination: Hospital Care Means States Pay Dearly. Pew Center on the States, February 28, 2012.

12   U.S. Census Bureau. Geographical Mobility/Migration, October 21, 2008. http://www.census.gov/population/www/socdemo/migrate.html.

13   Levinson, W., Roter, D., Mullooly, J, Dull, V. and Frankel, M. Physician-patient communication. The Relationship With Malpractice Claims Among Primary Care Physicians and Surgeons. Journal of the American Medical Association, February, 1997; 277:553-559.

14   Sack, Kevin. Doctors Say 'I'm Sorry' Before 'I'll See You in Court.' New York Times, May 18, 2008.

15   Mack, Eric. Pew: One-third Surveyed Prefer Texting to Talking. November 6, 2013. http://news.cnet.com/8301-17938_105-20108461-1/ pew-one-third-surveyed-prefer-texting-to-talking/.

16   Purcell, Kristen, Search and Email Still Top The List Of Most Popular Online Activities. Pew Internet & American Life Project, August 9, 2011.

17   Madden, Mary. Networked Workers. Pew Internet & American Life Project, September 24, 2008.

18   Statistic Brain. Facebook Statistics, November 18, 2013. http://www. statisticbrain.com/facebook-statistics

19   People Claim. The Review of Reviews, November 18, 2013. http:// www.peopleclaim.com/images/review-of-reviews-peopleclaim.jpg